SIGMA MALE EVOLUTION

Unveiling the 50 Key Personality Traits

Book 2
Dating Strategies

Book 3
Sigma Vs Alpha

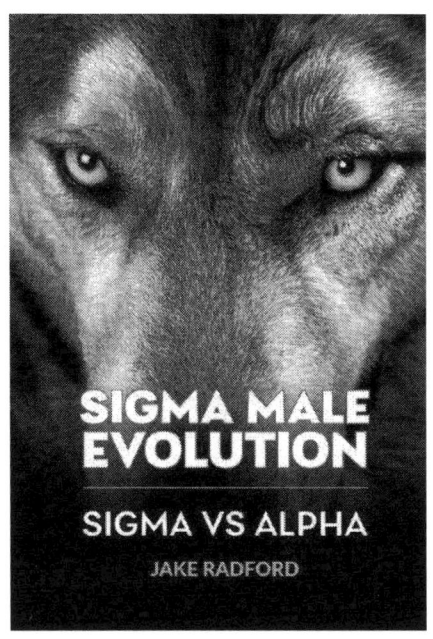

Preface

Greetings, thank you for picking up this book, "Sigma Male Evolution: Unveiling the 50 Key Personality Traits".

My name is Jake Radford, and I am a Sigma Male. You might be wondering what that means, and indeed, it's taken me a considerable part of my life to fully understand what it entails. It's a journey of self-discovery that has been fascinating, insightful, and at times, challenging.

Being a Sigma Male is not a choice one makes or a label one casually adopts; rather, it is an inherent identity that manifests in myriad ways throughout our lives. For me, it started with a feeling of being different, of not quite fitting into the traditional social structures and expectations. I often felt like an observer, a silent participant in the grand theatre of life, watching, learning, and evolving at my own pace, often contrary to the society's prescribed timeline.

Throughout my journey, I came to understand that my distinct perspective on life wasn't a hindrance or an anomaly, but a unique strength. As a Sigma Male, I found that my resourcefulness, my independent thinking, and my ability to thrive in solitude were not qualities to be hidden but to be embraced.

"Sigma Male Evolution: Unveiling the 50 Key Personality Traits" marks the beginning of an enlightening trilogy dedicated to the Sigma Male persona. This first book sets the foundation, unravelling the 50 key traits that define a Sigma Male. It aims to shed light on the complexities of this unique personality type, serving as an insightful resource for self-identified Sigma Males or those intrigued by this distinct personality archetype.

As we venture further into the trilogy, the upcoming books, "Sigma Male Evolution: Dating Strategies," and "Sigma Male Evolution: Sigma Vs Alpha," promise to delve deeper into the Sigma Male's approach to dating and his distinguishing traits from his Alpha counterparts. However, for now, our focus lies in laying a solid understanding of the Sigma Male personality.

Yet, for all its strengths, the path of the Sigma Male can be a solitary one. That's why I wanted to create a space where Sigma Males could connect, learn from each other, and foster a sense of community. This led me to establish *TheSigmaHub.com*, a platform dedicated to exploring and understanding the Sigma Male lifestyle.

On *TheSigmaHub.com*, you'll find a vibrant forum where Sigma Males from all walks of life share their experiences, challenges, and triumphs. The blog features a wide range of articles and resources designed to deepen your understanding of what it means to be a Sigma Male. It's an ongoing and collaborative effort, and I warmly invite you to join us in this journey.

By sharing this book, it's my hope that you'll find validation, understanding, and perhaps, a little guidance in your journey. Whether you identify as a Sigma Male or are simply curious about this unique personality type, I hope that you will find the insights in this book useful and inspiring.

Thank you once again for choosing this book, and for taking the time to read my words. It is a privilege to share this journey with you, and I look forward to hearing your thoughts and experiences as you delve into the pages that follow.

Warm regards,
Jake Radford

Contents

Preface 4

Introduction: Sigma Males - Charting Their Own Course 9

Part I: The Sigma Male Essentials 12

    Chapter 1: Mastery of Independent Thinking 13

    Chapter 2: Unwavering Confidence 15

    Chapter 3: Introversion as a Strength 17

    Chapter 4: Keenly Observant Nature 19

    Chapter 5: Embracing Self-Sufficiency 21

Part II: Building the Sigma Skillset 23

    Chapter 6: Resourcefulness as a Skill 24

    Chapter 7: Pragmatic Approach to Life 26

    Chapter 8: Disciplined Lifestyle 28

    Chapter 9: Autonomous Decision-Making 30

    Chapter 10: Unstoppable Ambition 32

Part III: Navigating Emotions & Intrigue 34

    Chapter 11: Art of Emotional Detachment 35

    Chapter 12: The Intrigue of Mysteriousness 37

    Chapter 13: High Perceptive Abilities 39

    Chapter 14: Resilience in the Face of Adversity 41

    Chapter 15: Analytical Problem-Solving 43

Part IV: Celebrating Individuality 45

    Chapter 16: The Courage to Be Non-Conformist 46

    Chapter 17: The Loner's Comfort 48

Chapter 18: Rational Decision-Making 50
Chapter 19: Flexible Adaptability 52
Chapter 20: Trusting Intuition 54

Part V: Embracing Privacy & Unpredictability 56
Chapter 21: Discretion and Privacy 57
Chapter 22: The Thrill of Unpredictability 59
Chapter 23: The Art of Finding Resources 61
Chapter 24: Open-Mindedness as a Virtue 63
Chapter 25: Unleashing Creativity 65

Part VI: Fostering a Sigma Mindset 67
Chapter 26: Strategic Life Planning 68
Chapter 27: The Philosophical Mind 70
Chapter 28: The Power of Self-Motivation 72
Chapter 29: Adventurous Spirit 74
Chapter 30: Harnessing Empathy 76

Part VII: Lifelong Learning & Lifestyle Choices 78
Chapter 31: Thriving as Independent Learners 79
Chapter 32: Minimalism as a Lifestyle 81
Chapter 33: Cultivating Patience 83
Chapter 34: Versatility in Skills and Interests 86
Chapter 35: The Power of Introspection 88

Part VIII: Privacy & Resilience 91
Chapter 36: The Value of Privacy 92
Chapter 37: Resilience in Solitude 94
Chapter 38: The Power of Observation 97
Chapter 39: Embracing the Unpredictable 100

Chapter 40: The Power of Solitude 103

Part IX: Independence & Reflection 106

Chapter 41: The Art of Observing 107

Chapter 42: The Silent Influencer 110

Chapter 43: The Non-Conformist 113

Chapter 44: The Self-Improver 116

Chapter 45: The Solitude Seeker 119

Part X: Continuous Self-Improvement & Presence 122

Chapter 46: The Non-Competitor 123

Chapter 47: The Self-Sufficient Individual 126

Chapter 48: The Mysterious Aura 129

Chapter 49: The Silent Influencer 132

Chapter 50: Adapting to Change - The Sigma Male Way ... 135

Conclusion: Sigma Male Traits - A Journey Towards Personal Mastery 138

Introduction: Sigma Males - Charting Their Own Course

We live in a world that often categorizes men into two archetypal roles - the alpha male, typically associated with leadership, dominance, and extroversion, and the beta male, often viewed as being more accommodating, submissive, and reserved. But what if there's another, less explored archetype that doesn't neatly fit into this binary? A type of man who is comfortable stepping out of societal norms and expectations, who is introverted yet assertive, independent yet impactful, and content in his solitude? This book is about that archetype - the Sigma male.

This comprehensive guide aims to delve deep into the concept of Sigma males, men who are self-reliant, introspective, and resilient. Through this exploration, we will not only discover the unique traits and behaviours that define them but also understand the transformative journey that one can embark on to embody these traits in their own lives.

In the following chapters, you'll be introduced to the core traits of the Sigma male. This is not a roadmap to becoming a Sigma male, but rather an exploration of a less-known archetype and the wisdom it offers. The aim is not to encourage you to fit into a specific mould, but to glean insights that resonate with you and enrich your personal growth journey.

We will delve into the Sigma male's approach to personal success, a perspective that deviates from conventional views. Instead of chasing external validation and societal recognition, Sigma males define success in their own terms, based on personal values and goals. Their measure of success lies not in the validation from others, but in the fulfilment, they find in their pursuits.

You will also uncover how Sigma males, despite their preference for solitude, can silently influence their environment. They may not be in the spotlight, but their actions, grounded in deeply held convictions, can inspire those around them and have a profound impact.

Resilience and adaptability are other key characteristics of the Sigma male that we will explore. Sigma males thrive in change and are skilled at adapting to life's challenges, using their resilience and flexibility to navigate the ever-changing landscapes of life.

However, this guide isn't merely theoretical; it provides actionable insights and relatable examples that will help you adopt these traits into your life. It's a journey towards self-improvement and personal mastery, encouraging you to explore solitude, cultivate introspection, define your own success, influence silently, and build resilience and adaptability.

As we explore the world of the Sigma male, remember that the goal is not to become a perfect archetype of a Sigma male, but to discover aspects of this archetype that resonate with you, and can help you live a more authentic and fulfilling life. Each chapter is an opportunity to reflect on how these traits can be integrated into your own journey, helping you to chart your own course, just as a Sigma male would.

Whether you identify with every trait of a Sigma male, or just a few, this book will provide valuable insights into personal growth, self-understanding, and authentic living. Through the lens of the Sigma male archetype, you will discover the power of introspection, the strength in solitude, and the satisfaction in self-reliance.

Welcome to an exploration of the Sigma male – a journey towards understanding the less-explored male archetype, and through it, your own path towards personal mastery and authentic living. Let's begin.

Part I: The Sigma Male Essentials

Chapter 1: Mastery of Independent Thinking

In the realm of personality archetypes, the Sigma male stands out in their Mastery of Independent Thinking. This trait is a beacon, illuminating their path to self-discovery and self-realization. Independent thinking doesn't just mean having thoughts of one's own, but the ability to scrutinize, analyse, and ultimately understand different perspectives before reaching conclusions.

Firstly, this characteristic allows Sigma males to view the world through an unfiltered lens. Instead of simply accepting societal norms or popular opinions, they deconstruct these conventions, examining their foundations and motivations. This isn't a rebellious act, but rather a journey to genuine understanding. For instance, where most people might blindly follow a trend, a Sigma male would question its origin, purpose, and impact. This introspective curiosity allows them to discern the essential from the ephemeral.

Secondly, Independent Thinking equips Sigma males with an unparalleled problem-solving ability. They see solutions where others see dead-ends. Their out-of-the-box approach is often the key to unlocking intricate dilemmas. Picture a Sigma male in a challenging work situation, where traditional methods have failed. Their independent thinking will inspire a novel solution, surprising others with its ingenuity.

However, a potential downside of independent thinking could be a sense of alienation. At times, Sigma males might feel detached, their ideas misunderstood or dismissed by those accustomed to conformist thinking. But, true to their nature, they turn this around positively, viewing it as an opportunity for growth. They understand that not everyone will comprehend their unique perspective. Instead of fostering resentment, they cultivate patience, and with time, they learn to articulate their thoughts better, bridging gaps and creating understanding.

The journey to harnessing this trait isn't always smooth. It requires courage to question norms and patience to weather the storm of misunderstanding. It isn't about contrarianism for its sake, but about pursuit of truth and wisdom. The process might involve reading widely to expose oneself to diverse ideas, practicing introspection, and developing a habit of questioning. Remember, the goal is not to alienate oneself, but to cultivate a deeper understanding of the world.

Embracing Independent Thinking means rejecting the comfort of the herd. Yet, it's through this path that the Sigma male finds his unique place in the world. They understand their individuality is not a cause for concern, but a sign of their authentic selves. The world may not always understand them, but it often comes to appreciate them. Their solutions, innovations, and ideas, born from their independent minds, can change the world, one thought at a time.

In the journey of mastering Independent Thinking, the Sigma male finds their own rhythm, dances to their own beat, and in this dance, they find a freedom that's uniquely their own. As we venture into the next chapter, we'll explore how this freedom intertwines with a trait that's just as compelling: Unwavering Confidence.

Chapter 2: Unwavering Confidence

An intriguing facet of the Sigma male persona is their Unwavering Confidence. Much like the North Star, this trait serves as a steadfast guide, a reliable beacon in their journey through life's unpredictable terrain. Unlike the brash arrogance sometimes mistaken for confidence, the Sigma male's assurance is rooted in a deep understanding of their capabilities and potential.

The first layer of their Unwavering Confidence lies in their acceptance of self. Sigma males accept who they are, with all their strengths and weaknesses, and this acceptance fuels their confidence. They do not seek external validation, nor do they crumble under criticism. They understand their worth and this understanding shields them from the fluctuations of societal approval. A Sigma male, for example, does not waver under peer pressure; they know their value isn't tied to the whims of the crowd.

Secondly, this confidence nurtures a resilience that enables them to face challenges head-on. They don't shy away from difficulties but perceive them as opportunities for growth. When faced with a hurdle, the Sigma male draws upon their inner strength, confident in their ability to surmount it. If they encounter a professional obstacle, they approach it strategically, their confidence fuelling their determination to overcome it.

Yet, one might argue that there could be a pitfall to such confidence, that it might border on arrogance or lead to overconfidence. Indeed, the line can be blurry. But this is where the Sigma male's self-awareness plays a crucial role. They are aware of this potential trap and consciously ensure that their confidence remains rooted, in their actual abilities rather than an inflated sense of self.

In transforming the possible negatives of overconfidence into positives, the Sigma male exercises introspection. They regularly evaluate their actions and decisions, recognizing their triumphs and acknowledging their mistakes. This reflective process keeps their confidence healthy and grounded, preventing it from turning into hubris.

Cultivating unwavering confidence isn't a task achieved overnight. It requires introspection, acceptance of oneself, and a positive, realistic assessment of one's abilities. Learning from failures, rather than getting disheartened, also plays a pivotal role in building this confidence. For the Sigma male, each setback is a steppingstone towards greater self-assurance.

In essence, the Unwavering Confidence of the Sigma male is a testament to their self-assured nature, their refusal to be swayed by external validation, and their courage to confront challenges. It's a confidence born not of arrogance but of a deep, unwavering knowledge of oneself. In the chapters that follow, we'll see how this confidence dovetails beautifully with other Sigma traits, creating a personality that's unique and compelling. Next, we delve into how the Sigma male transforms Introversion into a Strength.

Chapter 3: Introversion as a Strength

Within the intriguing enigma of the Sigma male lies the core trait of Introversion. Often misunderstood in a society that largely values extroverted traits, introversion is not a limitation but a significant strength for the Sigma male. It's their silent superpower, setting the stage for introspection, deep thinking, and meaningful connections.

Firstly, their introverted nature fuels their rich inner life. Sigma males have a realm within them, filled with ideas, questions, reflections, and dreams. Their introversion provides the space for these intellectual and imaginative pursuits. They are like an artist lost in their thoughts, weaving intricate tapestries of ideas. This deep inner life often leads to novel perspectives, innovative solutions, and profound insights.

Secondly, their introverted tendency propels them towards quality interactions. Sigma males may not be the life of the party, but they are the ones who engage in meaningful one-on-one conversations. They are the listeners, the ones who understand, empathize, and connect on a deeper level. These authentic relationships, albeit few, are incredibly rewarding. A Sigma male might not be surrounded by a huge social circle, but those who are in his life appreciate his depth and sincerity.

The challenge, however, lies in society's misunderstanding of introversion, often perceiving it as aloofness or indifference. But Sigma males, with their strong self-awareness, view these misconceptions as opportunities to redefine what introversion truly means. They understand their need for solitude is not a rejection of others, but a means to recharge, reflect, and delve deeper into their inner realm.

In turning the perceived negatives of introversion into positives, Sigma males embrace solitude as a tool for self-improvement and self-understanding. They use this time to nurture their mind, develop their skills, and foster a strong sense of self. With patience, they also learn to communicate their need for solitude to others, fostering understanding and acceptance.

Adopting this trait involves understanding one's energy pattern. Are social interactions draining, or do they energize you? Embracing introversion isn't about isolating oneself, but about finding the right balance between social interactions and solitude. For a Sigma male, this balance is key to harnessing the power of their introverted nature.

In conclusion, the Introversion of a Sigma male is a journey inward. It's a path that takes them to their intellectual depths, facilitates meaningful connections, and fosters an enriching solitude. In the following chapter, we will uncover how this introversion complements another fascinating Sigma trait: their Keenly Observant Nature.

Chapter 4: Keenly Observant Nature

A noteworthy trait that distinguishes Sigma males is their Keenly Observant Nature. It's as if they carry within them a secret lens, scrutinizing the world around them, peering beyond the superficial, and discerning the subtle details that often go unnoticed by others.

The first noteworthy aspect of this keen observation is their ability to understand people and situations deeply. Sigma males pick up on non-verbal cues, the slight change in tone, the briefest hesitation - details that provide insights into a person's thoughts and emotions. This equips them with a heightened sense of empathy, enabling them to connect more profoundly with others. Imagine a Sigma male in a conversation, where the other person struggles to express a complex emotion. Their keen observation will guide them to understand the unsaid, offering support or guidance that hits the mark.

Secondly, their observant nature is an invaluable tool in problem-solving. Sigma males observe patterns, detect anomalies, and foresee potential issues, their perceptiveness often leading to innovative solutions. For instance, in a project, they might identify a minor detail that could escalate into a significant problem, allowing for early resolution.

However, this constant observation and analysis could potentially lead to overthinking or an information overload. Here's where the Sigma male's innate ability to introspect steps in. They understand this pitfall and make conscious efforts to balance their observations with their need for mental peace. They discern when to observe and when to let go, turning what could be a negative into a positive.

Turning this trait into a strength requires deliberate cultivation. It begins with active attention to one's surroundings - the people, the environment, the unfolding events. It requires patience and quiet attentiveness. But it's equally essential to know when to disconnect, to prevent an overload. For the Sigma male, this equilibrium is crucial to harnessing their Keenly Observant Nature.

In essence, the keen observation of the Sigma male is not mere spectatorship; it's an active engagement with their environment, an exploration of the world and the people in it. It's through this engagement that they understand, empathize, foresee, and innovate, making their Observant Nature a key strength in their arsenal of traits.

As we navigate to the following chapter, we will delve into how this observant nature perfectly aligns with another essential Sigma trait: Embracing Self-Sufficiency.

Chapter 5: Embracing Self-Sufficiency

Integral to the Sigma male archetype is the profound trait of Embracing Self-Sufficiency. This characteristic, like an unseen force, propels them towards independence and autonomy, instilling in them a deep sense of self-reliance. Far from isolating them, this trait equips them with the capability to navigate life's intricacies with resilient self-confidence.

Firstly, self-sufficiency promotes autonomy in their personal and professional life. Sigma males, being self-reliant, are not dependent on external assistance for their needs or desires. They find the resources, solutions, and capabilities within themselves to achieve their goals. For instance, a Sigma male might teach himself a new programming language rather than relying on a tutor, utilizing his resources and demonstrating his self-sufficiency.

Secondly, self-sufficiency nurtures a strong sense of self-worth in Sigma males. Because they can depend on themselves, they recognize their strength and capabilities. They do not require external validation to affirm their worth; their confidence is rooted in their ability to handle life's challenges independently.

The potential negative aspect of self-sufficiency, however, is that it can lead to an aversion to seek help when needed, posing a risk of self-isolation. Sigma males, with their introspective nature and keen self-awareness, recognize this potential pitfall. They understand that self-sufficiency is not about shunning all outside help, but about knowing they have the capacity to stand alone when necessary.

To convert this potential negative into a positive, Sigma males strive for a balance between self-reliance and interdependence. They know when to tackle challenges independently and when to seek collaboration. In this way, they transform what could be a barrier into an opportunity for growth.

Embracing self-sufficiency is a journey towards independence, but it is not a journey one must undertake alone. It's about growing your skills, honing your abilities, and building confidence in your capabilities, but it's also about recognizing when collaboration and outside assistance can lead to better outcomes.

In conclusion, Embracing Self-Sufficiency is a cornerstone of the Sigma male persona. It empowers them, equips them, and elevates their self-worth. But it also teaches them the valuable lesson of balance. As we move forward to the following chapter, we will explore how self-sufficiency beautifully interweaves with another Sigma trait: Resourcefulness as a Skill.

Part II: Building the Sigma Skillset

Chapter 6: Resourcefulness as a Skill

Integral to the Sigma male's unique profile is their knack for resourcefulness. This innovative trait is their compass, guiding them through life's challenges with an intuitive sense of direction and an unyielding determination. More than just a skill, resourcefulness is the Sigma male's lifeline, bridging the gap between challenge and solution.

Firstly, Sigma males leverage their resourcefulness to tackle problems in unique ways. Their ability to think outside the box and utilize the resources at hand allows them to develop creative solutions. For example, a Sigma male stuck with a broken-down vehicle would not only manage to fix it but might even enhance its performance using available resources, demonstrating a quintessential case of resourcefulness.

Secondly, resourcefulness empowers Sigma males to adapt to changing circumstances swiftly. In an ever-evolving world, adaptability is key, and the Sigma male, with his resourceful mindset, thrives in the face of change. They see opportunities where others see obstacles, making the best of even the toughest situations.

However, there is a potential pitfall in being overly resourceful – it can lead to a reluctance to invest in long-term, sustainable solutions. Sigma males, with their introspective nature, are quick to identify this risk. They know that while being resourceful is important, it doesn't replace the need for consistent growth and improvement.

To turn this potential negative into a positive, Sigma males strike a balance between leveraging current resources and investing in future ones. They realize that resourcefulness is not just about solving today's problems but also about preparing for tomorrow's challenges.

Cultivating resourcefulness begins with adopting a solution-oriented mindset. One must learn to look at problems not as obstacles but as opportunities to innovate. For a Sigma male, this involves continuous learning, adaptability, and an unyielding resolve to overcome challenges.

In conclusion, Resourcefulness is a powerful tool in the Sigma male's arsenal. It fuels their problem-solving abilities, boosts their adaptability, and propels them towards uncharted terrains of potential. As we move forward to the next chapter, we will explore how this resourcefulness synergizes with the Sigma male's Pragmatic Approach to Life.

Chapter 7: Pragmatic Approach to Life

A defining characteristic of Sigma males is their Pragmatic Approach to Life. They're not merely dreamers lost in the clouds of idealism; they're also grounded realists who navigate life's complexities with sensible, practical solutions. Their pragmatic approach, like a sturdy anchor, keeps them steady amidst the unpredictable tides of life.

Firstly, their pragmatic mindset empowers them to make efficient decisions. Sigma males look at situations objectively, analyse the options available, and make choices that are feasible and effective. Consider a Sigma male planning a journey; he wouldn't just dream about the destination but would meticulously map out the most efficient route, prepare for possible obstacles, and have contingency plans ready.

Secondly, pragmatism enables Sigma males to adapt to unexpected changes. Life is unpredictable, but a Sigma male, with his pragmatic outlook, isn't easily swayed by sudden shifts in circumstances. They take changes in stride, adjusting their strategies and making the best out of even the most challenging situations.

However, there's a potential risk for pragmatism to stifle creativity and hinder the pursuit of seemingly unreachable dreams. Sigma males, with their introspective nature, recognize this risk. They understand that while pragmatism is a valuable trait, it should not confine their imagination or limit their aspirations.

To turn this potential negative into a positive, Sigma males balance their pragmatism with their dreams. They remain grounded, yet they're not afraid to reach for the stars. They know that pragmatism and dreams are not mutually exclusive;

instead, they work together to create a life of success and fulfilment.

Cultivating a pragmatic approach requires an understanding of reality, analytical thinking, and a knack for problem-solving. For a Sigma male, this involves observing their surroundings, understanding the rules of the game, and using this knowledge to navigate their path.

In conclusion, a Pragmatic Approach to Life is the compass guiding the Sigma male through the journey of life. It's their practicality, their adaptability, their unwavering rationality that enables them to face life's intricacies head-on. In the next chapter, we'll discover how this pragmatism seamlessly blends with another significant Sigma trait: A Disciplined Lifestyle.

Chapter 8: Disciplined Lifestyle

In the pantheon of Sigma male traits, one characteristic stands resolute – their adherence to a Disciplined Lifestyle. This trait, much like a rhythmic undercurrent, lends consistency and order to their lives, shaping their actions and decisions with a sense of deliberate purpose.

Firstly, a disciplined lifestyle facilitates goal-oriented action. Sigma males define clear objectives and persistently work towards them, unfazed by momentary distractions or short-term pleasures. Imagine a Sigma male committed to physical fitness. Despite a hectic schedule or inclement weather, he would not forsake his daily workout routine, embodying the quintessence of discipline.

Secondly, discipline enhances their self-control. This self-mastery empowers Sigma males to resist impulsive actions, aiding them in making thoughtful decisions that align with their long-term goals. For example, a Sigma male desiring financial security would refrain from frivolous spending, instead choosing to invest wisely for a secure future.

However, there's a potential downside to an overly disciplined lifestyle – it can lead to rigidity and a resistance to spontaneity. Sigma males, with their perceptive nature, recognize this danger. They understand that while discipline is key to achieving goals, life also requires flexibility and the capacity to adapt to changing circumstances.

To transform this potential negative into a positive, Sigma males balance their discipline with adaptability. They maintain a strict regimen, but they are also open to changes that life may usher in. They understand that discipline doesn't signify rigidity;

instead, it's a scaffold that supports their aspirations while allowing for necessary adjustments.

Cultivating a disciplined lifestyle involves setting clear goals, building consistent habits, and practicing self-control. For Sigma males, discipline is not a task; it's an integral part of their lives that aligns their daily actions with their long-term aspirations.

In conclusion, a Disciplined Lifestyle is a cornerstone in the Sigma male's life, moulding their actions and decisions, guiding their path towards their goals. As we transition to the next chapter, we will explore how discipline aligns with the Sigma male's Autonomous Decision-Making.

Chapter 9: Autonomous Decision-Making

A compelling element within the Sigma male's identity is their capacity for Autonomous Decision-Making. This attribute, like a rudder, helps them navigate the often-turbulent seas of life, enabling them to steer their course with confidence and unwavering resolve.

Firstly, autonomous decision-making allows Sigma males to chart their own path in life. They are not swayed by societal expectations or peer pressure; instead, they carve their own way based on their values and aspirations. For instance, a Sigma male, driven by his passion for art, might choose to pursue a career as an artist, rejecting conventional career paths, exemplifying the autonomy in his decision-making.

Secondly, this autonomy builds their self-confidence. Sigma males trust their judgment and rely on their instincts. They take ownership of their decisions, reinforcing their self-belief and bolstering their self-esteem. A Sigma male, after weighing all options, might decide to invest in an unconventional business venture. Whether it fails or flourishes, he embraces the outcome, knowing it was his decision.

However, there's a potential downside to autonomous decision-making - it can lead to isolation or an over-reliance on one's perspective. Sigma males, with their insightful nature, are quick to spot this risk. They understand that autonomy should not exclude the valuable input of others or prevent them from seeking advice when necessary.

To transform this potential negative into a positive, Sigma males balance their autonomy with receptiveness to others' viewpoints. They are confident in their decision-making abilities, yet open-minded enough to appreciate the wisdom that others bring. They realize that autonomous decision-making doesn't mean solitary decision-making, but rather a discerning blend of self-reliance and perspective-taking.

Cultivating autonomous decision-making involves developing self-awareness, trusting one's intuition, and learning from experiences. For a Sigma male, this not only bolsters their self-confidence but also shapes their identity, allowing them to build a life that truly reflects who they are.

In conclusion, Autonomous Decision-Making is a powerful compass in the Sigma male's journey, empowering them to take charge of their lives confidently. As we move forward to the next chapter, we will delve deeper into another significant Sigma trait that complements this autonomy – Unstoppable Ambition.

Chapter 10: Unstoppable Ambition

Residing deep within the Sigma male's core is a trait of Unstoppable Ambition. Like a mighty river coursing relentlessly towards the ocean, this attribute drives them forward, shaping their path with a potent mix of determination and resilience.

Firstly, unstoppable ambition fuels their motivation. Sigma males don't merely dream; they relentlessly pursue their aspirations, transforming thoughts into tangible reality. Picture a Sigma male with a vision to revolutionize technology. Despite the inevitable hurdles, his ambition drives him to tirelessly innovate, tirelessly push boundaries, tirelessly strive for his vision's realization.

Secondly, this burning ambition aids Sigma males in overcoming obstacles. Life often presents a multitude of challenges, but Sigma males, with their insatiable ambition, view these not as barriers but steppingstones on their journey to success. A Sigma male aiming for a major career breakthrough, for example, might face rejection multiple times. Yet, he perceives each setback as an opportunity for growth, driven by his unstoppable ambition.

However, there is a potential pitfall with this trait - it can lead to burnout or an unbalanced lifestyle. Sigma males, with their introspective nature, are astute enough to recognize this risk. They understand that while ambition is a potent driver, it should not compromise their overall well-being or eclipse other aspects of life.

To turn this potential negative into a positive, Sigma males temper their ambition with balance. They relentlessly chase their goals, yet they understand the importance of rest, of downtime, of moments spent in quiet introspection or joyous recreation. They realize that unstoppable ambition doesn't mean uncontrolled fervour but rather a sustained, balanced drive towards achieving their goals.

Cultivating unstoppable ambition involves nurturing a strong desire for success, resilient perseverance, and the ability to learn from failures. For a Sigma male, this powerful ambition is not just a trait; it's a beacon that illuminates their path, guiding them towards their dreams with unerring determination.

In conclusion, Unstoppable Ambition is a potent force in the Sigma male's life, driving them forward, shaping their journey, and propelling them towards their aspirations. As we proceed to the next chapter, we will explore how this unstoppable ambition seamlessly integrates with a key Sigma trait - the Art of Emotional Detachment.

Part III: Navigating Emotions & Intrigue

Chapter 11: Art of Emotional Detachment

In the intricate puzzle of the Sigma male's identity, one piece that often stands out is their mastery of the Art of Emotional Detachment. Like the calm at the heart of a storm, this trait equips them with the ability to maintain a tranquil inner state amidst the tumultuous whirlwinds of life.

Firstly, emotional detachment bestows upon Sigma males a degree of mental clarity. They are able to observe situations objectively, stripping away layers of emotional bias that might cloud judgment. Imagine a Sigma male faced with a complex problem at work. His ability to detach emotionally allows him to scrutinize the situation with clear, unobstructed vision, leading to effective problem-solving.

Secondly, this trait bolsters their resilience. Sigma males do not let setbacks or failures weigh heavily on their hearts. They learn from their mistakes without allowing negative emotions to hinder their progress. For example, a Sigma male who experiences failure in a business venture wouldn't wallow in self-pity or regret. Instead, he would calmly assess the situation, extract valuable lessons, and move forward.

Additionally, emotional detachment helps Sigma males maintain their independence. They are not easily swayed by the emotions of those around them. They can empathize with others, but they do not let external emotional turmoil affect their inner peace. In a heated group discussion, a Sigma male would remain a calm voice of reason, not succumbing to the collective emotional chaos.

However, there is a potential downside to emotional detachment – it could be perceived as aloofness or lack of empathy. Sigma males, with their profound self-awareness, understand this risk. They realize that emotional detachment should not hinder their ability to connect with others on a deeper, emotional level.

To turn this potential negative into a positive, Sigma males strive to balance their emotional detachment with genuine empathy. They maintain their emotional independence while also ensuring that they can understand and share the feelings of others. They realize that emotional detachment doesn't mean emotional unavailability, but rather a state of equanimity that allows them to handle emotional situations with grace and understanding.

Cultivating the art of emotional detachment involves developing emotional intelligence, mindfulness, and the ability to manage emotions effectively. For a Sigma male, this not only improves their ability to navigate complex situations but also contributes significantly to their overall well-being, establishing a foundation of emotional stability and resilience.

In conclusion, the Art of Emotional Detachment is an integral component of the Sigma male's psychological makeup, empowering them to traverse life's emotional landscapes with grace and poise. As we delve deeper into the Sigma male's world in the next chapter, we will explore another characteristic that perfectly complements emotional detachment – The Intrigue of Mysteriousness. This will reveal how Sigma males manage to maintain an air of intrigue while practicing emotional detachment, and how this combination of traits contributes to their unique allure.

Chapter 12: The Intrigue of Mysteriousness

In the vibrant palette of traits that compose the Sigma male's identity, a distinctive hue is their inherent mysteriousness. This attribute wraps them in an aura of intrigue, akin to a captivating novel whose pages invite exploration, yet whose full story is never easily discerned.

Firstly, the Sigma male's mysteriousness stems from their inherent preference for solitude. They thrive in their own company, enjoying the inner world of ideas and contemplations. Consider a Sigma male who prefers solitary activities such as hiking, painting, or reading. His companions might find his love for solitude perplexing, yet it is this very trait that contributes to his air of mystery.

Secondly, Sigma males aren't prone to disclose personal details or emotions readily, further enhancing their enigmatic allure. They might participate in a deep conversation about global issues or philosophical concepts yet steer clear of discussing their own personal experiences. This withholding of personal information creates a sense of curiosity in others, sparking an intrigue that is hard to ignore.

Thirdly, their unpredictable nature adds another layer to their mystery. Sigma males, with their autonomous decision-making, often make choices that surprise those around them. One moment, a Sigma male might be engrossed in a complex coding problem, and the next, he might decide to embark on a spontaneous road trip. This unpredictability is a cornerstone of their mysteriousness, leaving others guessing their next move.

However, their mysterious nature can lead to misunderstandings or even alienation. Others might misinterpret their aloofness as arrogance or their reticence as indifference. Sigma males, with their intuitive understanding of human nature, are well aware of this potential pitfall. They comprehend that while their mystery can be alluring, it should not deter meaningful connections with those who matter to them.

To transform this potential negative into a positive, Sigma males tactfully allow glimpses into their inner world, balancing their enigmatic nature with moments of openness. They understand that while maintaining their mysterious allure, they can also foster deep connections by sharing aspects of their lives and thoughts when they feel comfortable.

Adopting the trait of mysteriousness involves a delicate balance of maintaining personal space, discretion in self-disclosure, and unpredictability, while ensuring open communication and connection with others. A Sigma male navigates this balance with grace, making him an intriguing figure who commands attention without seeking it.

For example, a Sigma male in a social situation might maintain his mysterious allure by engaging in thoughtful conversation, revealing glimpses of his intellect and insight, yet refraining from divulging too much personal information. This creates an aura of intrigue around him, drawing others in, yet always leaving them with a desire to know more.

In conclusion, the Intrigue of Mysteriousness is a signature trait of the Sigma male, contributing significantly to their unique appeal. They masterfully maintain an intriguing balance between openness and discretion, captivating the curiosity of others. As we delve deeper into the next chapter, we will unravel the significance of High Perceptive Abilities, a trait that brilliantly complements their mysteriousness and enhances their ability to navigate their social and personal landscape.

Chapter 13: High Perceptive Abilities

In the myriad traits that comprise the Sigma male's complex persona, one of the most remarkable is their High Perceptive Abilities. This trait can be likened to an eagle's vision - sharp, keen, and capable of seeing what many might miss.

Firstly, high perceptive abilities bestow upon Sigma males an uncanny understanding of the world around them. They are adept at noticing subtleties and nuances that many might overlook. For instance, a Sigma male at a social gathering may effortlessly pick up on subtle shifts in the room's energy or read unspoken tensions between individuals that others might not perceive.

Secondly, this trait enhances their problem-solving skills. With their ability to observe and understand intricate details, Sigma males can view problems from multiple perspectives, facilitating innovative solutions. For example, a Sigma male working as a software engineer could leverage his perceptive skills to detect underlying patterns in code, leading to more efficient debugging and elegant code design.

Additionally, their high perceptive abilities extend to their understanding of people. Sigma males are often intuitive readers of human nature. They can sense underlying emotions, intentions, or motivations that aren't immediately visible. A Sigma male, for instance, could discern the genuine passion behind a colleague's seemingly routine presentation, allowing him to recognize potential allies in his professional journey.

However, this heightened perception could also present challenges. Being highly perceptive might make Sigma males more sensitive to environmental stimuli or emotional undercurrents, which can be overwhelming. They are aware of this potential downside and understand the need for balance.

To transform this potential negative into a positive, Sigma males learn to manage their high sensitivity. They might seek solace in solitude to process their observations or practice mindfulness to stay grounded amidst sensory or emotional overload. They understand that their keen perception, when balanced with self-care practices, becomes a valuable asset rather than a burden.

To cultivate this trait, Sigma males might engage in activities that sharpen their observation skills. A Sigma male, for example, might take up photography as a hobby. Framing the world through a lens could heighten his attention to detail, training his perception to notice the beauty in the mundane or the extraordinary in the ordinary.

In conclusion, High Perceptive Abilities are a defining trait of the Sigma male, enriching their understanding of the world and enhancing their problem-solving prowess. This quality, combined with their intriguing mystery, paints a compelling portrait of the Sigma male. As we move to the next chapter, we will delve into how Sigma males harness their resilience in the face of adversity, another powerful trait that, combined with their high perceptive abilities, makes them truly resilient warriors in life's arena.

Chapter 14: Resilience in the Face of Adversity

The Sigma male navigates through life like a ship, sailing fearlessly amidst storms, undeterred by the tumultuous waves. One of the key traits that enable them to traverse life's challenges with such grace is their Resilience in the Face of Adversity.

Firstly, Sigma males possess an inherent strength that allows them to bounce back from setbacks. They view adversity not as a deterrent, but as an opportunity for growth. Consider a Sigma male who has experienced a career setback. Rather than succumbing to defeat, he analyses the situation, learns from his mistakes, and sets sail once more, better prepared for the journey ahead.

Secondly, their resilience stems from their ability to maintain emotional equilibrium. Sigma males can detach themselves from emotionally draining situations, which allows them to view challenges more objectively. For instance, if a Sigma male faces criticism, he would dissect the feedback, absorb what is useful, and disregard any negativity, thereby strengthening his resilience.

Moreover, their resilience is fuelled by their autonomous decision-making. Sigma males trust their instincts and make choices based on their judgment. This independence allows them to adapt and overcome adversity. For example, a Sigma male might decide to quit a high-paying job to pursue a startup. Even amidst initial failures, his resilience drives him to adapt, learn, and continue striving towards his vision.

However, such resilience can sometimes be misconstrued as indifference or apathy. People might misunderstand their ability to detach from emotional situations or view their readiness to face adversity as an unwillingness to seek help. Sigma males, aware of this potential misinterpretation, make conscious efforts to communicate their intentions clearly.

To transform these potential negatives into positives, Sigma males learn to balance their resilience with emotional expressiveness. They understand that while resilience is key to overcoming challenges, expressing vulnerability is essential for forming genuine relationships. A Sigma male might share his struggles with a trusted friend or mentor, thus dispelling the notion of indifference and forging deeper connections.

Adopting resilience involves developing emotional balance, learning from setbacks, and nurturing independent decision-making. Sigma males could cultivate this trait by setting challenging goals and pursuing them, irrespective of obstacles. For instance, a Sigma male aiming to run a marathon could start training, gradually increasing his endurance, overcoming physical and mental barriers, thereby strengthening his resilience.

In conclusion, Resilience in the Face of Adversity is a key trait of the Sigma male, enhancing their ability to navigate life's challenges with grace and fortitude. This resilience, combined with their high perceptive abilities and intriguing mystery, equips them to thrive in life's diverse arenas. As we journey into the next chapter, we will explore their Analytical Problem-Solving skills, another potent trait that synergizes with their resilience to enhance their unique approach to life.

Chapter 15: Analytical Problem-Solving

Analytical problem-solving is yet another emblematic trait of the Sigma male, a facet that allows them to approach challenges and obstacles with a distinctive, strategic mindset. When faced with a dilemma, they aren't daunted; instead, they see it as an exciting puzzle waiting to be solved.

Firstly, Sigma males possess an innate ability to break down complex issues into manageable components. Their approach to problem-solving is often systematic and methodical. For instance, a Sigma male confronted with a business challenge would begin by dissecting the problem into various elements - market dynamics, competition, internal processes, and so forth. This segmented approach helps him to understand the problem more comprehensively and find targeted solutions.

Secondly, their analytical problem-solving ability stems from a knack for critical thinking. Sigma males tend not to take things at face value. They dig deeper, seeking underlying patterns, correlations, and causal relationships. Consider a Sigma male in a managerial role. Faced with declining team productivity, he wouldn't merely attribute it to lack of effort. Instead, he would analyse underlying factors such as work environment, communication practices, or personal issues affecting his team members.

Thirdly, Sigma males leverage their keen observational skills in their problem-solving process. They pay attention to details that might seem trivial but could hold the key to resolving the issue at hand. A Sigma male working as a detective, for example, might find clues in seemingly insignificant details at a crime scene, leading to a breakthrough in the case.

However, their analytical approach can sometimes be perceived as overly detached or unemotional. People may mistake their methodical, detail-oriented nature for indifference towards the emotional aspects of a situation. Furthermore, their propensity for deep analysis can lead to overthinking, which can result in decision paralysis.

Sigma males address these potential downsides by striking a balance between analysis and action, and by acknowledging the emotional facets of problems. They understand that not every problem can be solved by logic alone. Sometimes, intuition or empathy may lead to more holistic solutions. For instance, a Sigma male facing interpersonal conflicts in his team might need to use empathy and understanding in addition to logical analysis to resolve the issue effectively.

To cultivate this trait, one could practice logical exercises, puzzles, or engage in activities that require strategic thinking, such as chess. For example, a Sigma male wanting to hone his analytical problem-solving skills might take up chess. The game, with its emphasis on strategy and anticipation of the opponent's moves, would provide an excellent training ground.

In conclusion, the Analytical Problem-Solving ability is a distinctive trait of the Sigma male, offering them a unique lens to view and tackle challenges. This, coupled with their resilience and high perceptive abilities, sets them apart in the way they navigate life's labyrinth. As we proceed to the next chapter, we will explore their "Courage to be Non-conformist," another trait that synergizes with their analytical problem-solving to shape their singular identity.

Part IV: Celebrating Individuality

Chapter 16: The Courage to Be Non-Conformist

The Sigma male, ever the enigma, remains a mystery in the eyes of society, primarily due to their courage to be non-conformist. The freedom they find in carving their own path, unbound by societal expectations, is a signature characteristic that sets them apart from the rest.

Firstly, the Sigma male's non-conformity is expressed through their values and lifestyle choices. Unlike others who may pursue a high-profile career or a traditional life path, a Sigma male may choose to live nomadically, earning a living as a travel blogger, finding joy in new experiences rather than accumulating material possessions.

Secondly, their non-conformist nature extends to their thought processes. Sigma males often diverge from conventional thinking, questioning widely accepted norms and practices. For instance, a Sigma male might question traditional education systems, choosing instead to self-educate through a vast range of resources, arguing that this offers a broader, more personalized learning experience.

Thirdly, their courage to be non-conformist is embodied in their decision-making. Sigma males value their autonomy and rarely make choices based on external influence. For example, a Sigma male may choose to invest in an unconventional start-up, believing in its potential, despite others doubting its success.

However, this tendency to go against the grain can sometimes lead to isolation or misunderstanding from others who do not grasp the Sigma male's unique approach. Their unconventional decisions can be seen as risky or irrational, and their divergent thoughts can create conflict.

To mitigate these negatives, Sigma males balance their non-conformity with the wisdom to understand when conformity may be beneficial. They are not non-conformist for the sake of being different, but because they believe in the value of their unique path. When necessary, they can align with societal norms. For example, a Sigma male may conform to certain professional standards in his workplace, recognizing the importance of these norms in maintaining a conducive work environment.

Adopting this trait involves embracing one's individuality, questioning accepted norms, and making independent decisions. To foster this, Sigma males might engage in activities that stimulate independent thought, such as reading widely on various topics, practicing mindfulness to heighten self-awareness, or learning from diverse cultures through travel or research. For instance, a Sigma male wanting to embrace non-conformity might choose to spend a year traveling the world, gaining insights, experiences, and learning from the diverse ways of life.

In conclusion, the Courage to Be Non-conformist is a defining trait of the Sigma male, showcasing their audacity to diverge from the norm and embrace their individuality. Combined with their analytical problem-solving skills and resilience, this trait makes Sigma males adept at navigating the world on their own terms. As we delve into the next chapter, we'll explore another integral aspect of the Sigma male's persona - "The Loner's Comfort," which further illuminates their distinctive approach to life.

Chapter 17: The Loner's Comfort

Living comfortably in solitude is a characteristic that significantly defines a Sigma male. Their affinity for solitude, however, is not born from isolation or antisocial tendencies, but from a deliberate choice to value quality over quantity in their relationships and experiences.

Firstly, Sigma males thrive in solitude because it allows them the space for introspection. They cherish the quiet moments where they can delve deep into their thoughts and reflections. Take, for instance, a Sigma male who is a writer. He might opt to spend his weekends in quiet retreats, immersing himself in the tranquillity that fosters his creativity and thought process.

Secondly, Sigma males view solitude as an opportunity for personal growth and learning. They often utilize this time to acquire new skills, broaden their knowledge, or engage in creative pursuits. An artistically inclined Sigma male, for example, might use his alone time to master a new instrument, his progress marked not by accolades, but by his satisfaction.

Thirdly, their comfort in solitude stems from their independence and self-sufficiency. Sigma males don't need constant social interaction to feel contented. They find fulfilment in their pursuits and goals. A Sigma male entrepreneur, for instance, may prefer to work alone, relishing the freedom to make decisions without needing to reach a consensus.

Despite the many positives, the Sigma male's comfort in solitude can sometimes be misunderstood as aloofness or indifference. It could lead to missed opportunities for collaborative success or meaningful relationships. In extreme cases, it might even result in feelings of isolation or disconnection.

To counter these potential pitfalls, Sigma males intentionally cultivate a few close, meaningful relationships. They understand the value of connection and collaboration, recognizing when their solitude could transition into unhealthy isolation. For instance, a Sigma male might maintain a close-knit group of friends with whom he shares mutual respect and understanding, ensuring a balance between his solitary tendencies and social interaction.

For those looking to adopt this trait, it's crucial to understand that being comfortable in solitude does not equate to avoiding social interaction. Instead, it involves being at ease with oneself, valuing personal growth, and enjoying one's company. To cultivate this, engaging in solitary activities such as hiking, reading, or meditating could be beneficial. A Sigma male looking to explore the comfort of solitude might take up long-distance running, an activity that combines physical endurance with mental resilience and offers ample time for reflection.

In conclusion, The Loner's Comfort is a key attribute of the Sigma male, highlighting their independent spirit and self-sufficiency. This trait, when combined with their non-conformist nature and analytical problem-solving abilities, creates a unique persona that navigates the world with quiet confidence. As we turn to the next chapter, we delve into the Sigma male's "Rational Decision-Making" approach, a facet that works in harmony with their comfort in solitude to guide them through life's complexities.

Chapter 18: Rational Decision-Making

The Sigma male, navigating through life with an air of quiet confidence, demonstrates a unique characteristic that underscores their distinct persona: the trait of Rational Decision-Making. This attribute is central to their interactions, plans, and responses to the world around them, reinforcing their independent and introspective nature.

To begin with, Sigma males prioritize logic and reason in their decision-making process. They critically evaluate the available information, weigh the pros and cons, and consider the possible outcomes before reaching a conclusion. Consider a Sigma male entrepreneur faced with a significant business decision. He doesn't rely solely on instincts or external advice but dissects the data, analyzes market trends, and considers the long-term implications before charting his course.

Moreover, rational decision-making extends to their personal lives as well. Sigma males are not impulsive but take time to reflect before making choices, even in matters of the heart. They might consciously decide to remain single until they meet someone who aligns with their values and lifestyle, a decision stemming from careful contemplation rather than societal pressures.

Furthermore, Sigma males often apply a problem-solving approach to their decisions. They identify the problem, generate alternatives, evaluate these options, and implement the best solution. A Sigma male working in IT might approach a complex coding problem this way, methodically troubleshooting until he finds an effective solution.

Despite its many advantages, this rational approach may sometimes overlook the role of emotions and instinct, leading to perceived coldness or lack of empathy. Moreover, excessive analysis could lead to decision paralysis, stalling progress.

To counter these potential downsides, Sigma males integrate emotional intelligence into their decision-making process. They understand that while emotions should not dictate decisions, they provide valuable insight into their preferences and values. For instance, in a personal crisis, a Sigma male may consider both his emotional response and objective facts, striving for a decision that respects his feelings without compromising rationality.

Adopting this trait involves cultivating critical thinking, emotional intelligence, and problem-solving skills. To do this, a Sigma male might read books on logic and reasoning, engage in activities that enhance problem-solving skills, or practice mindfulness to improve emotional awareness. For example, a Sigma male wishing to improve his rational decision-making might engage in chess, a game that fosters strategic thinking and anticipates future scenarios.

In conclusion, Rational Decision-Making is a powerful tool in the Sigma male's repertoire, shaping their distinctive approach to life's various situations. It complements their solitary nature, non-conformity, and analytical skills, providing a framework for navigating their life journey. As we move to the next chapter, we will explore the Sigma male's "Flexible Adaptability", a trait that further enriches their unique approach to life and its diverse challenges.

Chapter 19: Flexible Adaptability

Flexible adaptability is a striking characteristic in the Sigma male's profile, emphasizing their ability to flow with life's unpredictability. They are not rigid in their ways; instead, they demonstrate a remarkable ability to adjust and adapt according to the circumstances.

To begin with, Sigma males excel at adjusting to new environments. They are not limited by their comfort zones, instead viewing new experiences as opportunities to learn and grow. A Sigma male who is a globetrotter, for instance, easily adapts to the cultures, cuisines, and languages of the places he visits, embracing the novelty rather than resisting it.

Secondly, Sigma males are proficient at adapting their plans when faced with unforeseen obstacles. They see such challenges not as setbacks, but as opportunities to devise innovative solutions. Consider a Sigma male who is an entrepreneur. Faced with an unexpected market downturn, he might reevaluate his business strategy, adapt his products or services to the current market demands, and discover new avenues for growth.

Additionally, Sigma males are flexible in their perspectives. They are open-minded and willing to adjust their views when presented with compelling evidence. This quality is particularly noticeable in discussions or debates where a Sigma male is involved. Rather than stubbornly sticking to his initial standpoint, he will consider all viewpoints and modify his opinion if the opposing argument is convincing.

Despite the numerous advantages of this trait, if not managed well, flexible adaptability might lead to indecisiveness or a lack of firm beliefs and values. Sigma males may also be misconstrued as fickle or inconsistent.

To mitigate these potential downsides, Sigma males ensure that their adaptability does not compromise their core values and principles. While they are flexible in their approach, they remain steadfast in their fundamental beliefs. For instance, a Sigma male working in a dynamic corporate environment may adapt to changing work trends and methodologies while maintaining his personal ethical standards.

For those seeking to cultivate this trait, the key lies in fostering an open mind, a willingness to step out of one's comfort zone, and the ability to handle uncertainties gracefully. Activities that expose one to new experiences or perspectives, such as travelling, reading broadly, or learning new skills, can be beneficial. For example, a Sigma male aspiring to enhance his adaptability might take up improvisational theatre, an activity that requires quick thinking, spontaneity, and the ability to adapt to unexpected scenarios.

In conclusion, Flexible Adaptability is a profound attribute of the Sigma male, complementing their other traits such as rational decision-making and comfort in solitude. This trait equips them with the agility and resilience needed to navigate the unpredictable currents of life. As we venture into the next chapter, we will uncover the Sigma male's innate ability to "Trust Intuition", a fascinating aspect that blends seamlessly with their flexible adaptability, enriching their unique life journey.

Chapter 20: Trusting Intuition

The Sigma male's journey is not only guided by conscious decision-making and flexible adaptability, but also by a profound Trust in Intuition. This characteristic taps into the individual's subconscious, deciphering non-verbal cues, patterns, and nuances that often escape conscious thought. It presents a fascinating interplay of the Sigma male's analytical and intuitive capabilities.

Sigma males often rely on their gut feelings in conjunction with rational thinking, whether in personal or professional life. They take note of those uncanny hunches, sudden inspirations, or strong instincts that spring up from their inner depths. For instance, a Sigma male entrepreneur might have a sudden intuitive leap about an innovative product idea that defies conventional market wisdom, but which he feels could be a game-changer.

In addition to relying on their intuition for inspiration, Sigma males often utilize it to assess people and situations. They have a knack for picking up subtle emotional undercurrents, unspoken intentions, or hidden dynamics, which aids them in their interactions with others. For instance, a Sigma male might intuitively sense discomfort in a friend who assures him everything is fine, leading him to probe deeper and provide the support his friend needs.

Moreover, Sigma males use intuition to navigate their own internal landscape. They use it as a compass, pointing towards what feels authentic and aligned with their true selves. This trust in their intuition can lead to choices that others might find unconventional but are perfectly suited to the Sigma male's unique path.

Despite these strengths, an overreliance on intuition can sometimes lead to impulsive decisions or misinterpretations, especially when unchecked by rational analysis. There's also a risk of appearing too unpredictable or inconsistent to others.

To mitigate these potential pitfalls, Sigma males balance their intuition with rational thought. They don't act on every gut feeling without also considering the facts at hand. This balance allows them to make well-rounded decisions that incorporate both instinctual and analytical elements. For instance, our entrepreneurial Sigma male might feel instinctively drawn to a new venture, but he will also ensure he conducts thorough market research and risk assessment before diving in.

For those aiming to cultivate this trait, it's about learning to listen to that quiet inner voice amidst the noise of external influences and distractions. This can be achieved through practices that promote mindfulness and self-awareness, such as meditation, journaling, or spending time in nature. A Sigma male wanting to improve his intuitive skills might adopt a daily meditation practice, fostering inner silence to better hear his intuitive whispers.

In conclusion, Trusting Intuition is a vital asset in the Sigma male's toolkit, adding depth to their rational and adaptable nature. It enhances their understanding of themselves and others and provides a rich source of inspiration and guidance for their unique path. As we move on to the next chapter, we will explore how the Sigma male values and practices "Discretion and Privacy", a trait that further emphasizes their self-reliant and introspective nature.

Part V: Embracing Privacy & Unpredictability

Chapter 21: Discretion and Privacy

In the constellation of the Sigma male's qualities, two stars shine with particular brightness: Discretion and Privacy. These traits, while often misunderstood, are critical to understanding the Sigma male's unique way of being in the world.

Sigma males are masters of discretion, embodying a sense of decorum and respect towards themselves and others. They have a natural inclination to keep their plans, emotions, and thoughts to themselves, sharing only when they feel comfortable and with those they trust. For instance, a Sigma male in a corporate setting might be working on an innovative project. Instead of broadcasting his ideas, he would work diligently behind the scenes until he's ready to present a well-rounded concept.

Discretion also manifests in their interactions with others. Sigma males respect the privacy of those around them, rarely prying into others' affairs unless invited to do so. They are the friends who will listen to your deepest fears and highest hopes, then lock them away in a vault of trust.

Privacy, another trait highly valued by Sigma males, goes hand in hand with their need for independence and introspection. The Sigma male cherishes his solitude, not out of antisocial tendencies, but as a space for reflection, creativity, and rejuvenation. A Sigma male writer, for example, would relish the peace of his private study, where he can dive deep into his thoughts and allow his imagination to run free.

Despite the many positive aspects of these traits, they may lead to misunderstandings or feelings of isolation if not balanced well. People may perceive Sigma males as aloof, secretive, or disinterested because of their reserved nature.

To navigate these challenges, Sigma males learn to strike a balance between their need for privacy and the necessity of social interaction. They may choose to communicate their need for solitude in a clear, compassionate manner to those around them to avoid misunderstandings. For example, our Sigma male writer might explain to his friends that his solitary retreats are not personal rejections but essential periods for his creative process.

Those who wish to cultivate these traits might want to set healthy boundaries in their lives. It involves learning to say no when needed, spending time alone regularly, and respecting others' boundaries as well. For example, a Sigma male working in a team might set clear boundaries about his work style, explaining that he prefers to ideate alone before coming together to discuss and fine-tune ideas.

In conclusion, Discretion and Privacy are cornerstones of the Sigma male's personality. They underpin their individualistic nature, nurture their introspective abilities, and form the bedrock of their interactions. In our exploration of the Sigma male's traits, we have delved into the mysterious depths and discovered a rich tapestry of attributes that set them apart. As we advance to the next chapter, we will explore the thrilling aspect of "The Thrill of Unpredictability", which sheds more light on the Sigma male's enigmatic aura.

Chapter 22: The Thrill of Unpredictability

In the realm of the Sigma male, a certain unpredictability reigns. Yet, it isn't chaotic or reckless. This trait, the Thrill of Unpredictability, is rather a dynamic blend of their deep self-knowledge, intuition, and adaptability, all forming a distinctive trail that defies traditional paths.

A Sigma male thrives on the thrill of unpredictability, often veering off beaten tracks in search of novel experiences or unconventional solutions. This can manifest in varied life domains, from their career paths to their personal interests. A Sigma male may, for instance, choose to become a digital nomad, relishing the uncertainty and spontaneity of living in different countries each year, instead of the traditional static lifestyle.

Their unpredictability can also be seen in their thought processes. Sigma males often surprise others with their unique perspectives and ideas, being able to think beyond traditional frameworks. This makes them excellent problem solvers and innovators. Imagine a Sigma male engineer, challenged with an insurmountable technical problem, who devises a solution that defies conventional thinking, yet is elegant and efficient.

Despite the thrill and advantages, the unpredictability can also present challenges. Being unpredictable can sometimes lead to misunderstandings or misinterpretations, as others might find it difficult to understand or keep pace with the Sigma male's shifting interests and ideas. It could also lead to periods of instability or risk-taking, which might not always result in positive outcomes.

To mitigate these potential pitfalls, Sigma males can balance their love for unpredictability with thoughtful planning and consideration. Even if they enjoy unpredictability, they are also aware of the need for stability and predictability in certain areas of life. Our digital nomad Sigma male, for example, might ensure he has a stable income stream and emergency savings to balance the uncertainties of his lifestyle.

For those wishing to cultivate this trait, it's about being open to new experiences, thinking outside the box, and embracing the unexpected. Developing a comfort level with uncertainty is key, which can be fostered by gradually pushing one's boundaries and exploring outside of one's comfort zone. The Sigma male engineer might constantly update his knowledge and skills, explore various disciplines, and engage in challenging projects to maintain his edge in innovation.

In conclusion, the Thrill of Unpredictability is another fascinating facet of the Sigma male's personality. It highlights their innovative, adaptable nature, and their comfort with the unknown, adding to their alluring aura. As we progress to the next chapter, we delve deeper into their resourceful nature in "The Art of Finding Resources", another intriguing aspect that contributes to the Sigma male's self-reliant and ingenious nature.

Chapter 23: The Art of Finding Resources

When we talk about Sigma males, a term often used in tandem is resourcefulness, particularly their knack for finding resources. It's not just about physical or tangible resources but extends to the realms of knowledge, ideas, and skills. They exhibit an uncanny ability to gather, and more importantly, utilize resources effectively to achieve their goals.

A Sigma male's resourcefulness might manifest in various scenarios. For instance, a Sigma male aspiring to learn a new language, instead of enrolling in a costly language course, might leverage free online resources, language exchange groups, and self-study techniques to master his desired language. He relishes the challenge of finding and assembling these resources into a coherent and effective learning plan.

Another manifestation of this trait is in their problem-solving abilities. Confronted with a complex issue, a Sigma male might sift through a plethora of information, discern the useful from the redundant, and apply it innovatively. Imagine a Sigma male software developer tasked with fixing a severe bug in a program. He might scour the depths of coding forums, experiment with different approaches, and ultimately come up with a solution that was overlooked by his peers.

However, there are potential pitfalls to this trait as well. Resourcefulness can occasionally tip over into obsessiveness, where the Sigma male could spend excessive time and energy in sourcing and gathering resources, leading to stress or burnout. It could also potentially alienate them from others if they overlook the opportunity to collaborate or seek help in their pursuit of self-reliance.

In balancing these challenges, Sigma males may learn to set boundaries on the time and energy spent on resource gathering and cultivate discernment to recognize when collaboration might be more beneficial than working solo. The Sigma software developer, for instance, might set a limit on how much time he spends trying to solve a problem on his own before asking for help or feedback from his peers.

For those looking to develop this trait, it's about nurturing curiosity, critical thinking, and a 'can-do' attitude. Begin by challenging yourself to find alternative solutions or sources for small tasks or problems. Over time, with practice, you will develop your resourcefulness and enjoy the sense of achievement and independence it brings.

In conclusion, the Art of Finding Resources is a vital aspect of the Sigma male's persona, underpinning their self-reliance and innovative problem-solving capabilities. It's not just about finding resources, but the joy they derive from the process, reinforcing their autonomy and resilience. As we navigate further into the Sigma male's world in the next chapter, "Open-Mindedness as a Virtue", we explore another key aspect that complements their resourcefulness and broadens their perspective.

Chapter 24: Open-Mindedness as a Virtue

Open-mindedness, a virtue cherished by the Sigma male, lends itself as the fundamental basis of their exploratory nature and their propensity for independent thought. They see the world not as fixed constructs but as a continually evolving puzzle to be interpreted, reinterpreted, and understood in new ways.

An open-minded Sigma male's narrative might begin by investigating unfamiliar topics, questioning established norms, and warmly embracing contrasting perspectives. Consider a Sigma male physicist, confronted with a novel theory that challenges established principles. Rather than dismissing it outright, he delves into the new concept, scrutinizes it, and even if he ultimately disagrees, he appreciates the fresh perspective it offered.

Open-mindedness is also evident in the Sigma male's personal life. They are willing to experiment with different lifestyle choices, hobbies, or philosophies, defying societal norms or expectations. For instance, a Sigma male might explore a minimalist lifestyle, reducing his possessions, and challenging the consumerist attitudes prevalent in society. This exploration is driven by a curiosity, a desire to experience life in its manifold forms, and not being bound by convention.

However, this trait is not without potential downsides. Being overly open-minded might lead to indecisiveness or confusion due to the sheer amount of possibilities considered. Additionally, their willingness to consider unorthodox ideas might sometimes isolate them from peers who hold more conventional views.

To counterbalance these challenges, Sigma males may practice discernment alongside their open-mindedness. They recognize that while all ideas can be considered, not all ideas are equally valid or beneficial. They also develop a keen sense of when to share their unconventional thoughts and when to maintain their mystique, depending on the context and the individuals involved.

To cultivate this trait, one might start by consciously exposing oneself to different perspectives, cultures, or ideas. This could be as simple as reading books from various genres or engaging in conversations with people from different walks of life. Over time, one can learn to not only tolerate but value differing viewpoints, thus deepening their understanding of the world.

In conclusion, Open-Mindedness as a Virtue further amplifies the enigma of the Sigma male. This trait enhances their curiosity, their love for exploration, and their ability to synthesize unique perspectives, contributing significantly to their charisma. As we proceed to the next chapter, "Unleashing Creativity", we'll observe how this open-mindedness paves the way for the vibrant creativity inherent in the Sigma male's persona.

Chapter 25: Unleashing Creativity

In the rich tapestry of Sigma male characteristics, creativity emerges as a brilliant thread, underpinning their unique worldview and distinctive problem-solving approach. Rooted in their open-mindedness and driven by their desire for self-expression, Sigma males are naturally inclined towards innovative thinking and creation.

Take the example of a Sigma male working as an architect. He's not content with following established styles or trends in his designs. Instead, he weaves together diverse architectural principles, sustainable practices, and a keen understanding of the environment to create structures that are both functional and aesthetically engaging. His designs stand out, not merely due to their novelty but because they mirror his individuality and his unique understanding of the world.

Creativity also fuels the Sigma male's passion for hobbies. Whether it's photography, painting, writing, or even cooking, Sigma males bring an inventive flair to their pursuits. For instance, a Sigma male chef might experiment with unconventional ingredient pairings, creating unique flavor profiles that turn a simple meal into an epicurean adventure. For him, cooking isn't merely about feeding; it's an act of creative expression, a testament to his inventiveness and curiosity.

However, there are potential pitfalls tied to this trait. There's the risk of their creativity being misinterpreted or undervalued by those who prefer convention over innovation. They may also face periods of self-doubt or creative blocks, which can be frustrating and potentially isolating.

To mitigate these challenges, Sigma males may learn to embrace the ebb and flow of the creative process, understanding that creative blocks are temporary and an integral part of the journey. They also develop resilience against external criticism, seeking satisfaction in their creative expression rather than external validation.

To cultivate creativity, one could start by stepping outside their comfort zones, exploring new areas of interest, and allowing their minds the freedom to wander and connect disparate ideas. Remember, creativity isn't about being an artist or an inventor; it's about perceiving the world in new ways and having the courage to bring these visions to life.

In conclusion, Unleashing Creativity is a fundamental aspect of the Sigma male's personality. It's the catalyst for their unique perspectives, their innovative solutions, and the unique way they engage with the world. As we delve into the next chapter, "Strategic Life Planning", we'll see how this creativity intertwines with their strategic mindset to guide their life's trajectory.

Part VI: Fostering a Sigma Mindset

Chapter 26: Strategic Life Planning

For a Sigma male, life isn't a sequence of random events, but a meticulously constructed narrative shaped by strategic planning. This approach, born from their love of autonomy and desire for self-fulfilment, serves as the compass guiding their actions and decisions.

Consider a Sigma male entrepreneur who dreams of establishing a tech startup. He doesn't rush into the venture impulsively; instead, he crafts a detailed strategy that includes market research, product development timelines, financing options, and contingency plans. This strategy isn't set in stone but evolves with changing circumstances, mirroring the Sigma male's adaptability and keen perceptive abilities.

In personal endeavours too, Sigma males exhibit strategic planning. For example, a Sigma male planning to master a musical instrument doesn't rely on sporadic practice sessions. Instead, he maps out a learning plan, sets achievable goals, schedules regular practice, and periodically assesses his progress. The result is not just proficiency in the instrument, but a deeper understanding of the process and the satisfaction of a plan well executed.

However, this tendency for strategic planning can lead to potential drawbacks. Overplanning might result in stress or paralyze them with over-analysis. Additionally, an overemphasis on planning can sometimes make them inflexible or unresponsive to spontaneous opportunities.

To balance these challenges, Sigma males need to remember that planning is a tool, not a rule. It is important to make room for spontaneity and the inevitable uncertainty that life presents. They can learn to see plans as flexible guidelines that can be adapted and revised as needed, rather than rigid frameworks that restrict their actions.

Cultivating this trait involves practicing foresight, developing patience, and honing problem-solving skills. One might begin by setting clear, realistic goals for different areas of life, then breaking these down into manageable steps, and finally committing to consistent action. Over time, strategic planning can become second nature, bringing clarity and purpose to their endeavours.

In conclusion, Strategic Life Planning is a defining attribute of the Sigma male, encompassing their independence, their desire for self-improvement, and their practical approach to life. In our journey into the next chapter, "The Philosophical Mind," we will see how this strategic planning is enriched by their profound introspection and thoughtful ponderings on life and existence.

Chapter 27: The Philosophical Mind

Delving into the depths of a Sigma male's personality, one finds a vibrant philosophical mind. Their natural inclination to introspection, coupled with their analytical problem-solving skills, empowers them to engage with abstract ideas and existential questions. The philosophical mind is not an auxiliary trait but rather a core part of the Sigma male's identity, shaping their worldview and influencing their decisions.

Consider a Sigma male who, instead of accepting societal norms at face value, chooses to question them. He ponders upon why things are the way they are, what gives life meaning, and how to lead a fulfilling existence. His quest for answers doesn't lead him to a predetermined destination but instead opens up new avenues of understanding and self-awareness.

In a professional context, the philosophical mind of a Sigma male allows them to approach tasks from a unique perspective. For instance, a Sigma male software developer doesn't just see code as a functional entity. He perceives it as a language, a form of expression, reflecting the programmer's mindset and approach. This philosophical outlook enables him to write more intuitive and creative code, setting his work apart from his peers.

Nevertheless, this philosophical tendency isn't without its challenges. There's a risk of overthinking, leading to decision paralysis or unnecessary worry. There's also the possibility of feeling isolated or misunderstood, as their profound insights might not resonate with others who prefer a more straightforward outlook.

To navigate these challenges, Sigma males must learn to balance their philosophical tendencies with practical considerations. They can allow their philosophical thoughts to enrich their lives rather than consume them. By sharing their insights with like-minded individuals, they can create meaningful connections and find validation for their unique perspectives.

To develop a philosophical mind, one could start by making time for introspection, questioning widely accepted beliefs, and reading philosophical literature. Moreover, practicing mindfulness can help keep their philosophical musings grounded in reality and prevent them from becoming overly speculative.

In conclusion, the Philosophical Mind is an integral part of the Sigma male's persona. It influences their understanding of the world, guides their decisions, and enriches their lives with depth and complexity. As we venture into the next chapter, "The Power of Self-Motivation," we will observe how the philosophical mind fuels the Sigma male's drive for self-improvement and personal growth.

Chapter 28: The Power of Self-Motivation

Within a Sigma male resides an inexhaustible source of drive that fuels his endeavours: self-motivation. Not reliant on external validation or praise, they find motivation from within, driven by their values, personal goals, and the joy of self-improvement. This trait, combined with their independent thinking and self-reliance, makes them incredibly self-sufficient and resilient.

Imagine a Sigma male writer who has been working on a novel. He doesn't need the promise of publishing success to keep him going, nor does he seek constant reassurance from others about the worth of his work. He writes because he loves to create, to express his ideas and to challenge himself. The process itself is rewarding, and each completed chapter is a testament to his self-motivation.

Similarly, in a professional context, a Sigma male project manager doesn't merely aim to meet the set targets. Instead, he finds motivation in optimizing the workflow, resolving complex issues, and leading his team towards efficient performance. The growth he experiences, the skills he develops, and the satisfaction of a job well done are his primary motivators.

Yet, the path of self-motivation isn't always smooth. There can be moments of self-doubt, periods of stagnation, or times when the motivation levels dip. Sigma males are also prone to putting high pressure on themselves, which may lead to burnout if not managed carefully.

To address these issues, Sigma males need to recognize that motivation isn't constant and it's natural for it to ebb and flow. They should learn to be kind to themselves during periods of low motivation, see these moments as opportunities for rest and rejuvenation rather than as failures. Turning challenges into learning experiences and negative thoughts into positive affirmations can help them keep their self-motivation healthy and sustainable.

Developing self-motivation involves setting personal goals that align with one's values and interests, cultivating discipline, and fostering a growth mindset. It's about finding joy in the journey and not just the destination. By focusing on personal growth and intrinsic rewards, one can nurture this empowering trait.

In conclusion, the Power of Self-Motivation is a significant trait that shapes a Sigma male's journey, enabling them to navigate life's challenges and pursue their passions with consistent drive and commitment. As we move into the next chapter, "Adventurous Spirit," we'll explore how their self-motivation fuels their desire for new experiences and learning opportunities.

Chapter 29: Adventurous Spirit

In the heart of a Sigma male resides a yearning for experiences that push boundaries and expand horizons – an adventurous spirit. Unlike the stereotypical image of a thrill-seeking adventurer, a Sigma male's concept of adventure is uniquely personal. It might manifest as intellectual curiosity, a passion for travel, or the courage to step outside their comfort zone in daily life.

For example, let's consider a Sigma male who has an insatiable curiosity about different cultures. He immerses himself in foreign languages, reads extensively about cultural histories, and travels whenever he can to experience these cultures first-hand. His adventurous spirit isn't satisfied with surface-level knowledge; he craves a deep, authentic understanding that can only come from direct experience.

In a professional setting, an adventurous Sigma male software engineer might continually seek new technologies and programming languages to learn. This drive for exploration enables him to stay ahead in his field and makes him an invaluable asset in a fast-paced, evolving industry.

However, embracing an adventurous spirit also implies welcoming uncertainty, and this can be daunting. Risks and setbacks are a part of any adventure, and Sigma males aren't immune to these challenges. They might also struggle with striking a balance between their need for solitude and their desire for exploration, as adventures often involve interacting with new people and environments.

To address these challenges, Sigma males need to view setbacks not as failures, but as learning opportunities. They should also understand that adventures can be tailored to their comfort levels – they don't always have to involve dramatic leaps into the unknown. Small steps, like learning a new skill or visiting a local place they've never been, can also feed their adventurous spirit.

To cultivate an adventurous spirit, one can begin by identifying areas of interest they'd like to explore, setting challenging yet achievable goals, and adopting a growth mindset. They should strive to see the world with curiosity and openness, valuing the journey as much as the destination.

In conclusion, the Adventurous Spirit is a fundamental facet of a Sigma male's persona, driving them to seek out new experiences and knowledge continually. As we progress into the next chapter, "Harnessing Empathy," we will explore how Sigma males balance their adventurous spirit with their ability to connect on a deep emotional level, adding another dimension to their rich and complex personalities.

Chapter 30: Harnessing Empathy

At the heart of a Sigma male's personality lies a trait that may not be immediately apparent, given their introverted nature - empathy. Their tendency towards solitude and introspection allows them to understand and connect with the emotions of others on a profound level. They aren't swayed by surface-level interactions; instead, they dive deep, perceiving the intricate emotional patterns that others might miss.

For example, imagine a Sigma male who works as a psychologist. He is particularly adept at listening to his patients and genuinely understanding their concerns. His empathetic abilities enable him to connect with their experiences, making him an exceptional psychologist capable of helping his patients navigate their psychological challenges.

Or, consider a Sigma male teacher who has a knack for understanding his students' unique learning needs. He senses when a student is struggling, even if they haven't verbalized their difficulty, and adapts his teaching approach accordingly. His empathy makes him not only an effective teacher but a cherished mentor.

Yet, empathy, as enriching as it can be, also has its potential pitfalls. Sigma males might find themselves taking on the emotional burdens of others, which can lead to emotional exhaustion. Their ability to feel others' pain deeply can sometimes be overwhelming, and their innate desire for solitude can be disturbed by the emotional turbulence.

However, like other challenges, Sigma males can navigate these issues with their characteristic resilience and introspective nature. They can learn to create emotional boundaries, recognizing that while empathy is a gift, it's also essential to protect their own emotional wellbeing. They can develop strategies to manage and balance their empathetic nature, such as mindful meditation, regular solitude, and selective engagement with emotionally draining situations.

To harness empathy as a positive trait, Sigma males can start by acknowledging the value it brings to their relationships and interactions. They can consciously exercise their empathetic abilities by listening actively, validating other people's feelings, and being there for them emotionally. By fostering an environment of understanding and acceptance, they not only enhance their own emotional intelligence but contribute positively to their surroundings.

In conclusion, while Sigma males are often misunderstood as aloof or detached, their quiet exterior houses a deeply empathetic heart. It's this empathy that allows them to form meaningful connections and positively influence those around them. As we venture into our next chapter, "Thriving as Independent Learners," we'll explore how Sigma males leverage their empathetic understanding to fuel their self-driven quest for knowledge and growth.

Part VII: Lifelong Learning & Lifestyle Choices

Chapter 31: Thriving as Independent Learners

An autonomous journey often serves as the bedrock of a Sigma male's life trajectory, and education forms a vital part of this exploration. With their self-sufficiency and unquenchable thirst for knowledge, Sigma males truly thrive as independent learners. Their solitary nature, coupled with an immense curiosity quotient, drives them towards self-education, breaking the conventional norms of the learning process.

Picture a Sigma male, a novice in the art of photography, setting out on an independent quest for mastery. He would invest time studying books, observing works of renowned photographers, experimenting with techniques, and learning from his mistakes. Over time, he would acquire proficiency, not through a formal classroom setting, but via the school of life.

Similarly, consider a Sigma male coder who started as a self-taught programmer. He began by learning from free resources available online and gradually honed his skills through constant practice, eventually becoming a successful software developer. Through his journey, he leveraged his keen observation and analytical skills, further sharpening his knack for independent learning.

Yet, this path is not without its challenges. Independent learning requires motivation, discipline, and the ability to face failure, aspects that may sometimes appear daunting. Moreover, lack of formal guidance could sometimes lead to learning gaps or missed opportunities for peer interaction and feedback.

Nevertheless, Sigma males are adept at turning these challenges into opportunities. The occasional failure becomes a stepping stone, and the lack of structured learning nurtures their innate creativity. They learn to use online forums, discussion groups, and mentor interactions to get feedback and enhance their knowledge.

For Sigma males aiming to excel as independent learners, it's crucial to adopt a systematic approach. Begin by setting clear learning objectives, creating a realistic plan, and sticking to it with unwavering dedication. Utilize available resources to the fullest - be it online courses, books, or peer networks. Practice what you learn consistently and maintain a growth mindset, knowing that each challenge faced is an opportunity to learn and grow.

In essence, the trait of thriving as independent learners is inherent in Sigma males. Their autonomy, combined with their inquisitive nature and self-discipline, makes them natural lifelong learners. This attribute not only equips them with diverse skills but also empowers them to navigate life on their own terms.

As we delve deeper into the next chapter, "Minimalism as a Lifestyle," we will explore how the Sigma male's tendency towards simplicity and functionality impacts their life choices and aids in their continual growth and self-development.

Chapter 32: Minimalism as a Lifestyle

An inveterate sigma male, the unassuming voyager of life, often appreciates the beauty of minimalism. For him, minimalism is not just a lifestyle choice, but a philosophical expression of his inherent nature - a testament to his desire for simplicity, autonomy, and the pursuit of true meaning.

Imagine a sigma male, standing before a vast landscape of consumerism, yet he chooses to be a minimalist. The reason isn't rebellion against the norm or a desire to be different, but a conscious choice driven by the love for simplicity and focus. He doesn't fill his life with superfluous possessions or distractions. Instead, he values experiences, knowledge, relationships, and anything that enriches his life at a fundamental level.

Consider the life of a sigma male who is an avid traveller. He carries only the essentials in his backpack, believing that traveling light frees him from the burdens of unnecessary possessions. His experiences on the road, the cultures he immerses himself in, and the people he meets enrich his life far more than an accumulation of material belongings ever could.

Similarly, visualize a sigma male who is a software developer, choosing to work remotely, and living a minimalist lifestyle. His home is sparsely furnished, his wardrobe essential, and his devices just enough to meet his needs. His life isn't filled with clutter but with open spaces that give him room to think, to create, to be. His choice of minimalism allows him to focus on his work, his learning, and his personal growth without distractions.

However, the path to minimalism isn't always smooth. The pressures of societal expectations, the lure of consumerism, and the human tendency to accumulate can create challenges.

There's also the misconception that minimalism means giving up all material possessions and living bare-bone, which may seem daunting and unrealistic to many.

Yet, the sigma male excels in turning the tide in his favor. Minimalism, for him, isn't about giving up everything but keeping what's truly important. By recognizing that the constant accumulation of material possessions often leads to clutter, both physically and mentally, he creates room for what truly matters. By doing so, he transforms the seemingly negative aspects of minimalism into a path of liberation.

For those aspiring to adopt this sigma trait, it's important to understand that minimalism is a personal journey. Start by identifying what's truly meaningful to you, what adds value to your life, and what aligns with your life goals. Then, declutter your life slowly, letting go of the non-essentials. Remember, the goal is not to live with the least amount but to make room for what truly matters.

The sigma male's preference for a minimalist lifestyle is a testament to his inner richness. By consciously choosing what to allow in his life, he affirms his independence and individuality. This trait greatly aids in their continual self-development and provides them with the clarity and focus to forge their unique path.

As we transition into our next chapter, "Cultivating Patience," we will delve into how this valuable trait, often overlooked in our fast-paced world, plays a vital role in the sigma male's journey and his interactions with the world around him.

Chapter 33: Cultivating Patience

In the labyrinth of life, the sigma male emerges as an enigmatic figure, often characterized by his remarkable ability to be patient. He seems to exist outside the conventional time-space continuum, not driven by the urgent frenzy that defines the modern world. Instead, he walks his path with a sense of timeless grace, appreciating the beauty of the journey rather than fixating on the destination alone.

Picture a sigma male as a chess player, surrounded by the intensity of the board, opponents, and onlookers. He sits with unwavering patience, his mind working on strategies, calculating possibilities, contemplating the moves of his opponent. He's in no rush, for he knows that the beauty of the game lies in its pace, in thinking and rethinking, and in making moves when the time is ripe. His patience is his strength, and it reflects in the quality of his decisions and eventually, his triumphs.

Now, imagine a sigma male as a photographer, waiting patiently for the golden hour to capture the perfect shot. His patience sets him apart, allowing him to immerse in the waiting, to observe the changing light and landscape, and to capture the magical moment when everything aligns. His art is a testament to his patience, an attribute that often separates the good from the great.

However, patience, like any virtue, does not come without its trials. In a world that worships speed, patience is often seen as a weakness. The sigma male, in his silent steadfastness, may be misunderstood as passive or indecisive. The value of patience may be underappreciated, and the need for immediate gratification might create conflicts.

Yet, the sigma male, with his characteristic aplomb, uses these challenges to reinforce his values. He understands that real growth takes time and that the path to mastery is often paved with patience. He turns the perceived negativity around by viewing patience as a bridge to achievement and personal growth. He appreciates that patience isn't just about waiting, but the ability to maintain a good attitude while waiting.

For those seeking to cultivate this sigma trait, it's crucial to understand that patience isn't about inactivity but about productive waiting. It involves working towards one's goals while also understanding that some things take time. It's about learning to tolerate discomfort, to handle delays and obstacles with grace, and to remain steadfast in the pursuit of one's ambitions.

One can cultivate patience by setting realistic expectations, practicing mindfulness, developing a resilient mindset, and appreciating the process rather than focusing solely on the outcome. Patience can also be cultivated by embracing uncertainties, by understanding that they are part of the human experience, and by learning to navigate them with composure and grace.

Patience is indeed a powerful attribute in the sigma male's toolkit. It's not just a trait but a lifestyle choice that empowers him to navigate the journey of life with grace, resilience, and dignity. It enables him to observe, understand, and act when the time is right, thus paving the path for his unique journey of self-discovery and growth.

In the next chapter, "Versatility in Skills and Interests," we will delve into another intriguing trait of the sigma male – his capacity for versatility. From his eclectic interests to his ability to adapt and learn new skills, the sigma male's versatility is a defining attribute of his enigmatic persona. As we journey forward, we'll explore how this trait contributes to his autonomous life path and how it can be harnessed by those who aspire to walk the sigma path.

Chapter 34: Versatility in Skills and Interests

The world of the sigma male is coloured with the rich hues of versatility. Much like a chameleon adapting to its environment, the sigma male demonstrates an uncanny ability to be multi-skilled, to diversify his interests, and to manoeuvre through life's varied situations with grace. His is a life of many layers, each revealing an exciting facet of his personality, a testament to his adaptability and his thirst for learning.

Consider a sigma male who, in one moment, is deeply engrossed in coding a new software, while in the next, he is strumming a melody on his guitar or engrossed in a historical novel. In one aspect of his life, he may be exploring the complexities of artificial intelligence and in another, appreciating the nuances of classical music. This inherent versatility allows him to traverse diverse fields with ease, making him a master of many trades.

Such versatility does not merely manifest in his interests or skills, but also in his approach to life. A sigma male can navigate various social contexts, adapt to changing circumstances, and switch roles as required. He could be a solitary thinker one moment, and a collaborative problem solver the next. This flexibility makes him a valuable team member and a formidable individual.

However, versatility can come with its set of challenges. Being interested in many things can sometimes lead to a lack of focus or direction. People may perceive the sigma male as inconsistent or indecisive. The sigma male may also face the struggle of balancing depth with breadth, of becoming a master of all trades or a jack of some.

Yet, the sigma male adeptly turns these potential negatives into positives. He understands that having varied interests enriches his life and expands his worldview. He sees the value in both specializing in a chosen field and diversifying his knowledge base. He manages his time effectively to ensure he nurtures his varied interests without compromising on his main focus areas.

To cultivate versatility, it's important to remain curious and open to new experiences. Try different hobbies, learn new skills, read broadly, and engage in a range of activities. Welcome opportunities to step out of your comfort zone. Embrace the process of lifelong learning and enjoy the journey of discovering new aspects of yourself and the world around you.

Another key aspect of fostering versatility is balancing between depth and breadth. It's not about learning everything but about having a sound understanding of varied subjects and the ability to delve deeper when required. Sigma males master this balance, becoming adept at acquiring new skills while continuing to improve their core competencies.

The sigma male's versatility sets him apart, highlighting his adaptability, his passion for learning, and his ability to thrive in various settings. It enhances his intellectual breadth, fuels his curiosity, and equips him to navigate the complexities of life with dexterity.

In the upcoming chapter, "The Power of Introspection," we will delve into how the sigma male harnesses the power of introspection to understand himself better, navigate life's challenges, and align his actions with his values. This inward-looking nature is a core component of the sigma personality, helping him navigate his solitary path with wisdom and resilience. Let's delve deeper into this fascinating trait and its role in the sigma male's journey.

Chapter 35: The Power of Introspection

In the depths of the sigma male's solitary existence lies a wealth of introspection. He frequently looks within, plunging into the profound reservoir of his thoughts, feelings, and motivations. His introspective nature allows him to scrutinize his inner world, enhancing his self-understanding and facilitating personal growth.

Imagine a sigma male, after a long day of engagements, retreating to his quiet corner. There, he reviews the day's occurrences, his actions, his emotions, and how they align with his values. In this reflection, he isn't merely replaying events; he's analysing them, seeking insights into his behaviour and that of others. It's through this lens of introspection that he derives wisdom and clarity.

Introspection can be a simple act, such as the sigma male sipping coffee in solitude while mulling over his thoughts, or a more structured process, like journaling or meditative practices. It is through such solitary activities that he unravels the complexities of his psyche, gains a clearer understanding of his values and beliefs, and charts the path of his personal evolution.

One sigma male may, for example, use introspection to understand his reactions to conflict. By analysing his responses, he may realize that his instinctive withdrawal stems from a fear of confrontation. Understanding this, he can work on effective strategies for conflict resolution, transforming his reflexive avoidance into thoughtful engagement.

The power of introspection, however, does not come without its challenges. Over-analysis can lead to excessive self-criticism and rumination, obscuring constructive self-reflection with clouds of self-doubt and negativity. Introspection may also be mistaken for self-absorption, creating a potential barrier to interpersonal connections.

Yet, the sigma male skilfully transforms these drawbacks into stepping stones. He understands that introspection is a tool for self-improvement, not self-destruction. He's mindful not to get lost in a maze of self-analysis, always anchoring his introspection to practical, positive action. He makes it a point to balance introspective periods with active participation in life, ensuring he remains connected to the world outside his mind.

Adopting this trait involves fostering a healthy introspective practice. It can be as simple as setting aside quiet time each day for self-reflection. Practices like journaling, meditation, and mindfulness can help provide structure and depth to introspection. It's important to remember, however, that introspection should serve to enhance understanding and foster growth, not to foster self-criticism or rumination.

Striking a balance between introspection and action is vital. Introspection should lead to growth and improvement, so always pair it with appropriate actions. If introspection reveals a certain behavioural pattern that needs change, devise a plan to address it. Apply the insights you gain from looking inward to your outward actions, ensuring your internal world and external life are harmoniously aligned.

In this way, the power of introspection becomes a compass for the sigma male, guiding him through the labyrinth of his inner world, illuminating his path, and helping him navigate his unique journey. It contributes to his growth, resilience, and depth, enriching his solitary existence with profound self-awareness and understanding.

In the following chapter, "The Value of Privacy," we will explore how the sigma male cherishes and protects his private space. We'll delve into how privacy acts as a sanctuary for him, facilitating his introspection, fuelling his independence, and fostering his unique identity. Stay tuned to understand the crucial role of privacy in the life of a sigma male.

Part VIII: Privacy & Resilience

Chapter 36: The Value of Privacy

Privacy, a fundamental aspect of the sigma male's character, holds immense value for him. Like a turtle retreating into its shell, the sigma male seeks privacy as a refuge, a haven for introspection, and a vital space for personal growth.

For the sigma male, privacy isn't merely about solitude. It's a realm where he can express his truest self, free from the judging gaze of others. In this realm, he can be his own audience, observing and learning about his own thoughts, feelings, and reactions. It's where he can recharge, refuel, and emerge renewed and invigorated.

Let's consider a typical day in the life of a sigma male. After a demanding day of work and social interaction, he retreats to his private space—a peaceful sanctuary, whether it be his room, a quiet corner in a park, or even a secret spot within his mind. Within this sanctuary, he finds peace and relaxation. Here, he can reflect, plan, dream, and grow without any external interruptions. It's a testament to his ability to find tranquillity within himself.

Privacy also plays a crucial role in the sigma male's creative endeavours. It is within the private confines of his space that the muse strikes, and ideas flow unhindered. For instance, a sigma male who is a writer might find his best ideas come when he's alone in his study, his thoughts the only sounds piercing the silence.

However, the sigma male's desire for privacy may not always be understood by others. It might be mistaken for aloofness or indifference, leading to potential misunderstandings in relationships. There's also a risk of becoming too withdrawn, of losing touch with the world outside his private sanctuary.

But the sigma male navigates these challenges with grace and wisdom. He knows when to extend the bridge between his private world and the world outside. He learns to communicate his need for privacy without appearing detached or aloof. More importantly, he maintains a healthy balance between his private and social life, ensuring he remains connected to others even while cherishing his solitude.

The road to adopting the sigma male's value for privacy begins with recognizing and respecting one's need for private space. It's important to establish a personal sanctuary—a physical space or a period of time—where one can retreat to for solace and self-reflection. This sanctuary can take any form, as long as it provides a sense of peace and privacy.

Communicating this need for privacy to others is equally crucial. A simple explanation can help prevent misunderstandings and ensure one's private space is respected. However, it's also important to maintain a balance, to prevent the protective shell of privacy from becoming a wall that disconnects one from others.

Privacy, for the sigma male, is more than just a preference—it's a necessity. It allows him the space to explore his inner world, to recharge, and to nurture his unique personality. Like the turtle that carries its home on its back, the sigma male carries his private sanctuary within him, providing a source of strength, comfort, and growth.

In the next chapter, "Resilience in Solitude," we will delve into another core trait of the sigma male—his ability to draw strength from his solitude. We will explore how solitude shapes his resilience and contributes to his unique identity. We will also discuss strategies to cultivate resilience and the power of solitude. Stay tuned to discover another compelling aspect of the sigma male's character.

Chapter 37: Resilience in Solitude

Like a lighthouse standing resilient amidst turbulent seas, the sigma male embodies resilience in solitude. This singular trait enables the sigma male to weather life's adversities with unflinching fortitude while thriving in his solitary existence.

A sigma male's solitude isn't a by-product of loneliness or social alienation. Instead, it is a conscious choice, a well-considered decision born from an understanding of oneself and the need for peace and self-sufficiency. Just like an eagle soaring solo through the sky, the sigma male finds his strength, courage, and resilience in solitude.

Take for example a sigma male entrepreneur. In his journey of setting up a successful venture, he encounters various challenges. There are moments of uncertainty, risks, and setbacks. But he doesn't falter or seek validation or support from others. Instead, he turns to his solitude. It's within this solitude that he finds his resolve, evaluates his strategies, learns from his failures, and bounces back with a stronger plan. This resilience, nurtured in solitude, becomes his ally in overcoming adversities and reaching the pinnacle of success.

Yet, resilience in solitude can sometimes be perceived negatively. Others might see the sigma male's solitary resilience as a sign of emotional detachment or indifference. But the sigma male doesn't let these misconceptions deter him. He understands that his resilience stems from his ability to stand alone, not from an unwillingness to engage with others.

The sigma male's resilient nature can sometimes also lead to excessive self-reliance, creating a reluctance to seek help even when needed. However, the sigma male is adaptable. He understands the potential downside of his trait and learns to reach out to others when necessary, without compromising his resilience. He recognizes that strength isn't just about weathering the storm alone but also about knowing when to seek shelter.

To cultivate resilience in solitude, one needs to first embrace solitude, not as a state of loneliness but as a space for personal growth and self-reflection. Spend time alone, free from distractions. Use this time to introspect, to discover your strengths and weaknesses, and to build your resilience.

Remember the entrepreneur? He didn't build his resilience overnight. It took time, self-reflection, and learning from his failures. Start with small challenges, learn from them, and gradually you'll be able to handle bigger adversities with fortitude and grace.

Communicating your need for solitude is equally important. Make it clear to those around you that your solitude isn't a sign of disinterest or alienation, but a personal space where you build your resilience. At the same time, learn to accept help when offered or needed. Resilience is not about handling everything alone but about knowing how to bounce back from adversities, even if it sometimes involves others' support.

The sigma male's resilience in solitude is not just about withstanding life's storms; it's also about coming out stronger and wiser. It's about using solitude as a tool to build inner strength, to reflect, to learn, and to grow. For the sigma male, solitude is a partner in resilience, a testament to his inner strength and ability to stand tall amid life's challenges.

In the next chapter, "The Power of Observation," we will delve deeper into the sigma male's keen observational skills. We will uncover how his penchant for observation contributes to his unique personality and how it guides him in navigating social and professional landscapes. We will also provide useful strategies for enhancing your observational skills, so stay tuned to explore another fascinating aspect of the sigma male's character.

Chapter 38: The Power of Observation

As the backdrop of a bustling world unfolds, one figure quietly stands apart, watching, learning, and understanding the patterns and nuances invisible to most - the sigma male. Known for their observation prowess, sigma males keenly perceive the subtleties of the world around them. This is a trait that sets them apart and gives them an edge in diverse situations, from personal interactions to professional decision-making.

Consider a sigma male working in a corporate environment. Amid the hustle and bustle of everyday work life, he doesn't just hear conversations; he listens and observes. He notices the unspoken communication, the nonverbal cues - a co-worker's hesitant tone, a manager's assertive body language, or a team member's discomfort during a discussion. With this understanding, he knows when to intervene, when to offer help, and when to step back. His observational skills serve as his secret weapon in navigating his professional life effectively and empathetically.

Sigma males often prefer to stay on the periphery in social settings, not because they shy away from interactions, but because it allows them to observe and understand people and situations better. It's this ability to observe without being centre stage that allows the sigma male to interpret the world in ways others may miss.

However, this trait can sometimes lead to sigma males being misunderstood. People may see their observational silence as disinterest or aloofness. The sigma male, however, does not let this deter him. He knows that his power lies in his silent observation, in understanding people beyond their words, and in interpreting situations beyond their surface.

Yet, a sigma male's intense observation can sometimes lead him to overthink or become overly critical. He may observe and analyse to the point of creating scenarios in his mind that may never occur. But the true strength of a sigma male lies in turning his potential weaknesses into strengths. He learns to control his tendency to over-analyse and leverages his observational skills to constructively critique and improve, rather than to overthink or worry.

To cultivate the power of observation, it's essential to train the mind to be present, attentive, and mindful. Practice active listening, pay attention to non-verbal cues, and try to understand what's not being said.

Take inspiration from the corporate sigma male mentioned earlier. He didn't develop his observational skills overnight. He practiced. He started by observing small team meetings, paid attention to body language, tone of voice, and conversation dynamics. Over time, he was able to understand his colleagues better and could use his observations to make informed decisions and actions.

However, do remember that observation isn't about judging or creating assumptions about people or situations. It's about understanding, empathizing, and making informed decisions. It's also important to balance observation with participation. Observing can provide insights, but it's through participation that one can put those insights into action.

Moreover, convey your observational nature to those around you. Let them know that your silent observation isn't indifference but your way of understanding the world better. Be open to explaining your perspective, and people will start to appreciate your observational skills rather than misunderstand them.

A sigma male's power of observation is an inherent part of his personality, a trait that makes him unique and insightful. By observing and understanding, he navigates the world with a depth of understanding that is seldom seen. And with his observations, he moves through life with a wisdom that is uniquely his own.

In the upcoming chapter, "Embracing the Unpredictable," we will explore the sigma male's ability to handle uncertainty and unpredictability. We will discover how this trait helps him thrive in unpredictable circumstances and what strategies he uses to embrace the uncertain. So, get ready to unravel yet another facet of the enigmatic sigma male.

Chapter 39: Embracing the Unpredictable

In a world of constant change, amidst the oscillating waves of the predictable and unpredictable, stands the figure of a sigma male. He is unfazed by the storm of uncertainty, and his inherent adaptability enables him to embrace the unpredictable with a poise that is truly remarkable. His trait of thriving in uncertain circumstances is not just commendable but also a cornerstone of his persona.

Imagine a sigma male entrepreneur who has ventured into a dynamic business landscape. As market trends fluctuate and new competitors emerge, he doesn't falter. He does not cling to a rigid plan. Instead, he adapts, evolves, and moulds his strategies in response to the changing scenario. When a new competitor disrupts the market, he doesn't panic. Instead, he observes, understands, and innovates to stay ahead. When his business model hits a roadblock, he doesn't get flustered. He reflects, revises, and comes up with an evolved model that aligns better with the current market dynamics. This ability to adapt and thrive in uncertain situations is what makes him successful as an entrepreneur.

In personal situations too, the sigma male thrives in unpredictability. In an unpredictable situation, such as a sudden change in plans or an unplanned journey, he doesn't stress or scramble to regain control. Instead, he goes with the flow, adapts to the new plan, and makes the most of the unexpected circumstances. This makes him an excellent companion in adventurous and spontaneous situations.

Nevertheless, the sigma male's embrace of unpredictability is sometimes misconstrued as inconsistency or a lack of commitment. People may question his shifting approaches or judge his spontaneous decisions. Yet, the sigma male remains unperturbed. He realizes that his adaptability is his strength, not a flaw. His ability to change, to let go of rigid plans, and to embrace the new is what allows him to thrive in life's unpredictability.

But this trait also comes with its challenges. The continuous flux of unpredictability can sometimes lead to exhaustion or the feeling of being adrift. It's crucial then for the sigma male to find his grounding amidst the change. This could be through regular introspection, maintaining a few constant routines, or having a set of core values that guide him. This way, he can continue to embrace unpredictability without losing his sense of self.

Adopting this trait of embracing unpredictability involves a shift in perspective. Rather than viewing unpredictability as a threat or a source of anxiety, see it as an opportunity for growth and learning. Cultivate adaptability. Like the sigma entrepreneur, when faced with an unexpected challenge, instead of panicking, pause, understand the situation, and adapt your approach.

Remember, it's okay to change your plans, to alter your path, to revise your strategies. It's not a sign of inconsistency, but a reflection of your ability to adapt and thrive in changing circumstances. Regularly stepping out of your comfort zone can also help you become more comfortable with unpredictability. Start small – it could be trying a new cuisine, picking up a new hobby, or traveling to an unfamiliar place.

Communicating your adaptability to others is also essential. Let them know that your adaptability is not a lack of commitment but a strength that enables you to handle diverse situations effectively. This will not only help you avoid misunderstandings but will also inspire others to embrace unpredictability.

Embracing unpredictability is not about carelessly drifting with the wind; it's about being flexible yet grounded, spontaneous yet thoughtful, adaptable yet consistent in values. It's about thriving in the dance of life where the only constant is change.

As we move into the next chapter, "The Power of Solitude," we will delve into how the sigma male thrives in solitude and uses it as a powerful tool for personal growth and self-discovery. Stay tuned as we uncover another exciting facet of the sigma male's journey.

Chapter 40: The Power of Solitude

Amid the social chatter, the constant pressure to engage, and the noise of society, the sigma male finds strength and clarity in solitude. He chooses to step away from the crowd, not out of fear or disdain, but because he cherishes his own company. His solitude is neither a sign of loneliness nor an escape; it is a space where he truly comes into his own.

Picture an artist, a sigma male, who cherishes his hours of solitude, for it is in these quiet moments that his imagination takes flight. As he stands before the blank canvas, he hears the voice within, guiding his hand, creating a world of colours that mirrors the depth of his inner universe. It's not that he doesn't enjoy social engagements or gatherings; he participates when he wants to. But his creative sparks are ignited in the solitude, where he can hear the whispers of his inner muse.

Or consider a sigma male explorer, who embarks on solo expeditions into the wild. As he treads through dense forests, climbs lofty peaks, or gazes at the star-studded sky, he finds solace in the embrace of nature. His solitary journeys are not escapes from society, but adventures where he discovers himself amidst the grandeur of nature. The lessons he learns, the insights he gains, and the transformation he undergoes are testaments to the power of solitude.

Despite its strength, the sigma male's preference for solitude often becomes a subject of misunderstanding. Society may see him as aloof, antisocial, or even eccentric. But the sigma male does not let these misconceptions sway him. He knows the value of solitude, the energy it infuses, and the perspective it provides. However, he is also aware that a complete retreat into solitude can create a sense of isolation or disconnection.

This is where the sigma male's characteristic of self-improvement comes into play. He balances his need for solitude with healthy social interactions. He nurtures a few close relationships, where he can be his authentic self. He participates in social activities that align with his interests and values. This way, he enjoys the benefits of solitude without sliding into isolation.

To adopt the sigma male's trait of valuing solitude, one needs to start by creating pockets of alone time. It could be as simple as savouring a cup of coffee in the morning silence, taking a solitary walk in the park, or dedicating an hour to a personal hobby. Remember, this is not 'wasted' time. It is an opportunity to connect with yourself, to hear your own thoughts, and to nurture your inner world.

Embrace the silence that comes with solitude. It is in these silent moments that the best ideas emerge, the deepest insights are revealed, and the most profound healing happens. Don't rush to fill the silence with distractions. Let it unfold, let it speak, let it guide.

It is also important to communicate your need for solitude to others. They may not understand initially, but being open about your preference for solitude will help them respect your space and your choices.

Keep in mind that solitude does not mean isolation. Like the sigma male, balance your solitary time with meaningful interactions. Nurture a few close relationships where you can be your authentic self. Engage in social activities that you genuinely enjoy.

In solitude lies the power to dive deep into the self, to engage with one's thoughts, to kindle one's creativity, and to nurture one's inner world. It is not an escape, but an exploration. An exploration that allows the sigma male to discover himself, to cultivate his strengths, and to navigate the journey of life with wisdom and clarity.

As we delve into the next chapter, "The Art of Observing," we will explore how the sigma male's keen observational skills become a tool for understanding the world and shaping his journey. We will discuss how these skills can be honed and integrated into our daily lives, thus adding another piece to the puzzle that is the intriguing sigma male.

Part IX: Independence & Reflection

Chapter 41: The Art of Observing

Behind every sigma male's subtle presence is an active observer. This ability to keenly observe their surroundings, people, and situations forms the core of their quiet strength. This trait doesn't make them simply passive spectators but gives them a nuanced understanding of the world that often goes unnoticed by others.

Imagine a chess player, a sigma male, who sits silently across the board from his opponent. As he carefully observes each move, he doesn't just see a piece moving from one square to another. He reads into the strategy, understands the intent, and anticipates the possible outcomes. His silent observation translates into powerful moves that take the opponent by surprise.

Picture a sigma male who is a psychologist. As he observes his clients, he is not merely noting their words. He reads between the lines, identifies patterns, and understands their emotions. His observations help him to decode their experiences, understand their perspectives, and guide them towards self-discovery and healing.

Yet, the sigma male's skill of observation can sometimes be misunderstood. They may come across as detached or unresponsive, leading to misconceptions about their intent or feelings. It's important to understand that their observant nature does not reflect indifference or lack of emotion. Rather, it's their way of engaging with the world, understanding it, and interacting with it on their terms.

Being observant, the sigma male is aware of this misinterpretation. He knows that while his observational skills serve him well, they can sometimes create a wall between him and others. So, he works on finding a balance. He combines his ability to observe with the ability to communicate. He shares his insights, offers his perspectives, and lets others see the world through his observant eyes.

To adopt this sigma trait, one must cultivate the habit of being present and attentive. In an era where distractions are just a click away, staying focused and attentive is a challenge, yet a necessity. It's not about simply watching or hearing; it's about understanding and interpreting. It involves being in the moment, whether it's a conversation, a task, or simply observing a sunset.

It's also about questioning and reflecting. When observing a situation, ask yourself: "Why is this happening?" "What led to this?" "What does it mean?" Reflect on your observations, draw connections, and deepen your understanding. Observing is not passive; it's an active and engaging process.

Remember, observing also includes observing yourself. Pay attention to your thoughts, emotions, and reactions. Understand your patterns, your triggers, and your strengths. Self-observation not only increases self-awareness but also aids in self-improvement.

Lastly, balance your observational skills with communication. Share your observations and insights with others. This will not only enrich your interactions but also help others understand your observational nature. Be aware that your keen observation might be misunderstood. So, express yourself, share your insights, and let your observational nature be a bridge, not a barrier.

The sigma male's power of observation offers him a unique perspective on life. It equips him with insights, understanding, and wisdom that is often overlooked by others. However, he also understands the need to balance this skill with communication and participation. After all, life is not merely to be observed but to be experienced and shared.

As we transition to the next chapter, "The Silent Influencer," we'll delve deeper into how the sigma male, with his silent presence and subtle actions, can become a powerful influence in both personal and professional life. We'll explore how this silent influence works, its advantages, and how one can cultivate this unique sigma trait.

Chapter 42: The Silent Influencer

In the bustling dynamics of our society, it's often the loudest who get the most attention. Yet, nestled within this hubbub, there exists a powerful, silent influence that belongs to the sigma male. His is a quiet presence that doesn't need to shout to be heard, nor does it seek the limelight to shine. This influential trait is something intrinsic to the sigma male, and it's a fascinating combination of silent authority, perceptiveness, and unspoken charisma.

Consider a scenario where a team is struggling with a complex problem at work. Among them, there's a sigma male, sitting quietly, observing, and processing the situation. He isn't vocal about his ideas, but when he finally speaks, his words are clear, concise, and packed with insight. This not only resolves the issue at hand but also leaves a profound impact on his teammates. He doesn't command the room with volume but with the weight and value of his words.

Or envision a sigma male in a social gathering. He doesn't seek the center of attention, rather preferring the edges, quietly observing and subtly interacting. Yet, his calm demeanor, insightful remarks, and authentic interest in others draw people towards him. He becomes the silent anchor in the whirlwind of social interaction.

However, it's worth mentioning that wielding silent influence isn't without its challenges. Often, in a world that celebrates extroverted characteristics, the sigma male's quiet nature might be misconstrued as aloofness or indifference. The very trait that makes them influential may also cause them to be misunderstood or overlooked.

Recognizing this, the sigma male turns this potential disadvantage into an opportunity for growth. He understands that communication is key in making his silent influence more accessible to others. He learns to articulate his thoughts more openly, balancing his introspective nature with a willingness to express himself. By doing so, he brings others into his world, allowing them to appreciate his quiet influence.

Adopting the trait of silent influence requires a conscious shift in one's approach. It's about embracing the quiet strength within and understanding that influence doesn't necessarily require loudness or extroverted charisma. Start by valuing your thoughts and ideas. Your insights are unique and valuable, and it's important to recognize this.

Silent influence also relies heavily on active listening. By showing genuine interest and understanding towards others, you build rapport and trust, thereby increasing your influence. When you do speak, make sure your words are thoughtful and meaningful. Quality always wins over quantity in the realm of silent influence.

It's also crucial to develop your non-verbal communication skills. A significant part of silent influence comes from how you present yourself. Your body language, facial expressions, and even your silence can speak volumes. A confident posture, an understanding nod, or a thoughtful pause can have as much impact as spoken words.

Finally, remember to balance your silent influence with open communication. It's essential for others to understand your thoughts and insights. Don't hesitate to express your ideas and opinions. This not only enhances your influence but also allows others to appreciate your unique perspective.

In the sigma male, we find a fascinating paradox. His silent influence, far from making him invisible, actually makes him more noticeable. His quiet strength and introspective nature attract people, instilling a unique form of leadership and authority that doesn't rely on volume or showmanship.

As we continue our exploration of sigma traits, we will move onto the next fascinating characteristic in the following chapter: 'The Non-Conformist.' Here, we will delve into how the sigma male's refusal to blindly follow societal norms serves as an essential aspect of his identity and how this can be both a challenge and a strength. We will also explore how to cultivate this trait and use it as a powerful tool for personal growth and authenticity.

Chapter 43: The Non-Conformist

In a world that so often pushes us towards conformity, the sigma male chooses a different path. With an unwavering commitment to authenticity, he stands as a non-conformist, challenging norms and societal expectations to carve out his own distinct identity. This intriguing trait of non-conformity forms the backbone of the sigma personality, manifesting as an unyielding desire to stay true to himself and his values.

To gain a deeper understanding, let's visualize the sigma male in a professional setting. There's an established protocol for how projects are managed, ideas are presented, and decisions are made. Yet, the sigma male, rather than blindly adhering to the status quo, asks why. Why should we follow these practices if there are better, more efficient ways available? He doesn't hesitate to challenge existing norms if they don't align with his understanding or values. His proposals may initially unsettle his colleagues, accustomed to the routine, but it's hard to ignore the logic and novelty of his ideas. This non-conformist approach not only promotes innovation but also redefines the boundaries of possibility.

In personal relationships too, the sigma male remains committed to his non-conformist nature. He doesn't indulge in pretence or change his behaviour to fit in or please others. Suppose there's a social gathering where everyone is discussing the latest popular show that he hasn't watched. The sigma male won't fabricate interest or opinions to join the conversation. He would rather stay true to his preferences, perhaps initiating a discussion on a topic he genuinely enjoys.

However, the path of non-conformity is fraught with challenges. Societies often view non-conformists with scepticism or even hostility. The sigma male may face criticism, exclusion, or misunderstanding because of his refusal to abide by societal expectations. But what others see as a hurdle, he views as an opportunity for growth. He learns to express his differing opinions respectfully and constructively, fostering understanding and respect among his peers. He turns potential alienation into an opportunity for enriching conversations and connections.

For those who aspire to adopt this trait, the first step is self-awareness. Understanding your values, interests, and preferences is key to developing non-conformity. Regular introspection can help you uncover these aspects of your identity. You might start by setting aside a few minutes each day for reflection, jotting down thoughts about your experiences and observations.

The next step is building the courage to express your authentic self. This could mean voicing a unique idea in a meeting, choosing a hobby that's not popular among your friends, or standing up against a practice you believe is unfair. Remember, non-conformity is not about rebelling without a cause but about remaining authentic.

Developing a strong sense of self-worth is also crucial. Understand that your value does not depend on others' approval. You have the right to your perspectives and preferences, even if they don't align with the majority. Building this mindset might involve working on self-esteem and practicing self-compassion.

Finally, embracing non-conformity means learning to navigate the challenges it brings. This involves developing effective communication skills to articulate your viewpoints and building resilience to handle potential backlash. Remember, the goal is not to alienate others but to create a space where diverse thoughts can coexist.

The non-conformist sigma male is a beacon of authenticity in a world often masked with pretence. His courage to challenge norms and be himself inspires others to explore their identities, promoting a culture of diversity and acceptance. Yet, he doesn't wear his non-conformity as a badge of honour or rebellion; it's simply his way of honouring his true self.

As we delve further into the world of the sigma male in the next chapter, 'The Self-Improver,' we will explore how the sigma's commitment to personal growth forms an integral part of his personality. We will look at the motivations behind this relentless pursuit of improvement, the challenges it brings, and the strategies to cultivate this trait. So, as we leave the realm of the non-conformist, we prepare to step into the mind of the self-improver, where we'll discover another layer of the enigma that is the sigma male.

Chapter 44: The Self-Improver

The sigma male is an archetype characterized by self-reliance, introspection, and most importantly, a constant pursuit of personal growth. This trait of self-improvement is intrinsic to his nature. His thirst for knowledge, development, and betterment of himself is unquenchable, making him a lifelong learner and self-improver.

Let's visualize a sigma male in his professional life to grasp this trait better. He is not the one to settle for mediocrity or stagnation. He constantly seeks to expand his skills, improve his strategies, and strive for excellence. For instance, as a software developer, he wouldn't just stick to what he learned in college or his early career. He would continually educate himself on new programming languages, modern algorithms, or advanced techniques. He would take up certifications, attend seminars, or participate in coding challenges to hone his abilities. His approach to self-improvement isn't limited to his core work; he might learn about project management, effective communication, or leadership principles, seeing the value in holistic growth.

In personal realms too, the sigma male's dedication to self-improvement shines brightly. He's the person who would set personal goals for fitness, learn a new language, or pick up a new hobby, not for external validation, but for his pleasure and growth. He values the journey of learning, relishing each step of progress he makes.

However, self-improvement doesn't mean that the sigma male is dissatisfied with who he is. On the contrary, it stems from a place of self-love and the understanding that growth and change are parts of life. His pursuit is not about attaining perfection but about continually evolving and becoming a better version of himself.

The road to self-improvement is not always smooth. It requires discipline, commitment, and often means stepping out of one's comfort zone. It may involve dealing with failures, setbacks, and criticism. But the sigma male perceives these not as obstacles but as opportunities to learn and improve. His resilience and dedication propel him forward on his journey of growth.

So, how does one cultivate the trait of self-improvement?

Begin with introspection. Understand what you want to improve in yourself. It could be a professional skill, a personal habit, or an aspect of your character. Having a clear idea of your improvement areas forms the foundation of your self-improvement journey.

Once you've identified your goals, create a structured plan to achieve them. Establish specific, measurable, achievable, relevant, and time-bound (SMART) goals. For instance, instead of vaguely deciding to "get fit," aim to "run a 5k in under 30 minutes by the end of three months." A structured plan gives you a clear path to follow and makes your journey more manageable.

Seek knowledge and resources to aid your improvement. Use books, online courses, mentors, or any reliable source to learn and grow. Don't hesitate to ask for help or guidance when needed. Remember, seeking assistance is not a sign of weakness but an essential part of learning.

Cultivate discipline. Consistency is key in self-improvement. Make your goals part of your daily routine. Whether it's practicing a new skill, reading a chapter of a book, or working out, consistency will lead to progress.

Learn to handle setbacks positively. On your journey, you will encounter challenges and failures. Instead of letting them discourage you, use them as learning opportunities. Analyze what went wrong and how you can improve in the future. Developing a growth mindset will help you turn obstacles into stepping stones.

Lastly, celebrate your progress. Self-improvement is a journey, and every small step forward is worth acknowledging. Reward yourself when you achieve a goal or reach a milestone. It will boost your motivation and make your journey more enjoyable.

In the upcoming chapter, 'The Solitude Seeker,' we will delve into how the sigma male finds solace and strength in solitude. We'll explore how this trait helps him in his journey of self-improvement, and how it shapes his unique way of engaging with the world. As we continue to unravel the sigma male's personality, each trait offers a unique perspective, adding to the intricate tapestry of this fascinating personality type. Stay tuned as we explore further.

Chapter 45: The Solitude Seeker

A defining characteristic of the sigma male is his preference for solitude. Unlike the extroverted alpha who thrives in social scenarios, or the beta who is usually comfortable being part of a group, the sigma often prefers his own company. This doesn't mean he is shy or socially awkward; rather, he often finds solitude to be more fulfilling and productive. In this chapter, let's delve into the sigma male's solitude-seeking nature and explore how you can cultivate this trait.

Imagine a bustling office setting. The alpha male is typically at the centre, leading meetings, making decisions, and enjoying the limelight. The beta male might be working in a team, collaborating and communicating effectively. But where is the sigma male? You'll likely find him working quietly in a corner, engrossed in his project, thinking deeply, and producing quality work. He thrives in this space of solitude and it's here that he does his best work.

In his personal life too, the sigma male values his alone time. He might spend it pursuing a hobby, reading, learning a new skill, or simply reflecting on his thoughts and experiences. Solitude for the sigma male is not about isolation, but about using this time for self-growth, introspection, and relaxation.

The solitude-seeking sigma male appreciates the quiet, which provides an environment conducive for deep thought and creativity. In this tranquillity, he can hear his own thoughts more clearly, understand his feelings, and plan his actions with greater precision. It allows him space to problem-solve without interruptions, to explore new ideas, and to create without distraction.

Now, how can one cultivate this solitude-seeking trait?

Firstly, understand the difference between loneliness and solitude. Loneliness is a negative emotional state where you feel alone and isolated. Solitude, on the other hand, is a positive, voluntary state where you enjoy spending time alone. To become a solitude seeker, you should learn to enjoy and value your own company.

Create a solitude routine. Dedicate a specific part of your day for solitude. It could be early morning when the world is still quiet, or late at night when everything has settled down. Use this time for activities that you love or that contribute to your self-improvement. It could be reading, writing, meditating, or simply reflecting on your day.

Understand that seeking solitude doesn't mean cutting off social connections. You can still maintain healthy relationships while valuing your alone time. It's about finding the right balance between social interaction and solitude.

Create a personal space conducive to solitude. It could be a quiet corner in your house, a personal study, or even a spot in your local park. This place should be where you can be alone with your thoughts without being disturbed.

Finally, see solitude as a journey of self-discovery. It is during these moments of quiet that you can dig deeper into your thoughts, feelings, and beliefs. You can use this time to get to know yourself better, understand your strengths and weaknesses, and work on your personal growth.

In the next chapter, 'The Non-Competitor,' we'll explore another intriguing trait of the sigma male: his lack of interest in competing for social dominance or approval. While society often measures success through competitive victories, the sigma male creates his own definition of success. How does this trait contribute to his uniqueness? And how can one adopt this non-competitive approach to life? Stay tuned as we continue to unravel the complex and captivating world of the sigma male.

Part X: Continuous Self-Improvement & Presence

Chapter 46: The Non-Competitor

A key characteristic of the sigma male that sets him apart from other archetypes is his lack of interest in competition for social dominance. Unlike the alpha male, who typically seeks the highest position in any social hierarchy, or the beta male, who often tries to fit in and win approval from others, the sigma male steers clear of such competition. He defines success on his own terms and is content to stand apart from the crowd. In this chapter, we will delve into this non-competitive nature of the sigma male and provide ways to adopt this unique trait.

In a corporate setup, imagine a typical scenario where a promotion becomes available. The alpha male would generally be the first to put himself forward, striving to outperform his peers and grab the opportunity. The beta male, on the other hand, might be hesitant but will eventually muster up the courage to participate in the competition, driven by the desire to fit into the societal norms of success. However, the sigma male is unlikely to be swayed by such opportunities unless it aligns with his personal goals and interests. He doesn't measure his worth by his rank in the corporate ladder but by his own metrics of success.

Let's take a school setting as another example. In a highly competitive environment where everyone is vying for the top spot, the sigma male would be the one calmly focusing on his interests and skills. While others are competing for grades or popularity, he is honing his unique talents, building his knowledge base, and defining his own success. It's not that he doesn't care about achieving; instead, he prefers to chart his own path and isn't concerned about the typical markers of success that others pursue.

Now, how can one cultivate this non-competitive nature?

Firstly, understand the difference between healthy competition and competing for social approval. While healthy competition can push you to improve, constantly competing for social approval can be exhausting and unfulfilling. As a sigma male, you should focus on personal growth and self-improvement rather than seeking external validation.

Develop a clear understanding of your interests, passions, and goals. Sigma males are usually driven by a strong sense of self-awareness. They know what they want and don't let societal expectations sway them. Spend time understanding yourself and what you truly want from life. This will help you stay focused on your path and prevent you from getting caught in the rat race.

Learn to value your own success metrics. Society often defines success in terms of wealth, position, and power. However, sigma males understand that success can have different meanings for different people. You might define success as leading a balanced life, achieving mastery in a particular field, or making a difference in the world. Whatever your definition of success, learn to value and pursue it.

Finally, cultivate a sense of contentment and self-validation. A key aspect of the sigma male's non-competitive nature is his ability to find contentment within himself. He doesn't need a trophy, a promotion, or social approval to feel successful. Learn to validate yourself, to take pride in your achievements, and to find satisfaction in your progress.

In the next chapter, 'The Self-Sufficient Individual,' we'll delve into the sigma male's self-sufficiency. Unlike the alpha or beta male who often relies on others for support or validation, the sigma male thrives on his independence and ability to take care of himself. How does this self-sufficiency contribute to the sigma male's unique persona, and how can you cultivate this trait? We'll explore these questions and more as we continue to unravel the intricate world of the sigma male.

Chapter 47: The Self-Sufficient Individual

The sigma male's non-conforming nature is often backed by an equally intriguing trait – self-sufficiency. His contentment with solitude, combined with his capacity to meet his needs without external help, results in a high degree of independence. In this chapter, we'll discuss how self-sufficiency shapes the sigma male archetype and provide actionable ways to cultivate this valuable trait.

To begin with, let's clarify what being self-sufficient means. In the context of the sigma male, it signifies his ability to sustain himself emotionally, mentally, and often physically, without relying heavily on others. This does not mean he avoids social interactions or disregards the value of relationships. Rather, he doesn't depend on others for his happiness, success, or well-being.

For example, consider a situation where an individual must relocate to a new city for work. A typical person might find this transition quite challenging – being away from family and friends, needing to establish new social connections, adjusting to a new environment, etc. However, a sigma male would approach this situation differently. He sees it as an opportunity for growth and exploration. The absence of familiar faces would hardly daunt him; instead, he would find solace in his solitude, explore the city at his own pace, and gradually make acquaintances if and when he feels the need.

In another instance, imagine facing a personal crisis such as a breakup or job loss. Many people rely heavily on their social circle for emotional support during such times. They seek solace in shared experiences and external validation. While there's nothing wrong with this, the sigma male handles such situations differently. He tends to rely on his internal resources, processing his emotions independently and taking time to rebuild his life on his terms.

So, how can one cultivate this trait of self-sufficiency?

First and foremost, start by developing emotional independence. This involves understanding your emotions, learning to manage them effectively, and not letting them be excessively influenced by others. It's about finding happiness within yourself and not basing it on external factors. Techniques like mindfulness, meditation, and journaling can aid in developing emotional independence.

Next, focus on enhancing your problem-solving skills. Sigma males are often adept at handling challenges because of their ability to find solutions independently. You can cultivate this ability by challenging yourself with different tasks, learning new skills, and stepping out of your comfort zone regularly.

Financial independence is another crucial aspect of self-sufficiency. While this might seem obvious, it's worth emphasizing given its role in enabling personal freedom. Aim to have control over your financial situation. This doesn't mean you have to earn a six-figure salary, but you should aim to live within your means and have a financial safety net.

Building resilience is also key to self-sufficiency. Life will inevitably throw curveballs at you, but being able to bounce back from adversities makes you stronger and less dependent on others. Developing a positive mindset, focusing on what you can control, and learning from failures can help build resilience.

Lastly, value your solitude. Sigma males are often introverted and draw energy from spending time alone. Use your alone time to engage in activities you love, introspect, and plan your life on your terms. This not only increases self-awareness but also fosters self-sufficiency.

In the next chapter, titled 'The Mysterious Aura,' we will discuss another fascinating trait of sigma males – their mysteriousness. Unlike the alpha's dominance or the beta's conformity, the sigma's aura is enigmatic, drawing others towards him even without intentional effort. How does this mysteriousness manifest, and how can one develop such an aura? Stay tuned as we continue our exploration into the world of the sigma male.

Chapter 48: The Mysterious Aura

A common thread that binds all sigma males is the aura of mystery that surrounds them. Unlike their alpha counterparts, who often rely on assertiveness and overt dominance, sigma males fascinate others with their enigmatic nature. It is their paradoxical blend of self-containment and unspoken charisma that attracts curiosity and intrigue. Let's delve into the essence of this trait and discover ways to foster an air of mystery, while still being true to ourselves.

The mysterious aura of a sigma male springs from his distinct lifestyle and mindset. Preferring solitude, they engage sparingly in social events, making each appearance intriguing to observers. Furthermore, sigma males rarely share personal details gratuitously, revealing aspects about themselves gradually, and often only when asked. This selective disclosure creates an allure, triggering interest and curiosity among others.

Think of a co-worker who consistently delivers exceptional work but is rarely seen participating in office gossip or happy hour. When this individual does join a team outing or share a personal story, people tend to listen with heightened interest. Their occasional engagement, combined with their preference for solitude, makes their presence more impactful, enhancing the aura of mystery around them.

Or consider the appeal of a famous author who shies away from the public eye, rarely giving interviews, and letting their work speak for itself. Their reticence doesn't push away their audience; rather, it draws them in, making people more eager to know about the mind behind the captivating stories.

To cultivate this mysterious aura, one must first value their privacy and become comfortable with solitude. Embrace time spent alone for self-reflection, personal growth, or simply enjoying your hobbies. This does not mean isolating oneself, but rather balancing social interactions with quality alone time.

Next, be intentional about the personal information you share. This doesn't advocate for dishonesty or evasiveness but emphasizes thoughtful disclosure. Consider what you reveal in conversations, on social media platforms, or any public forums. Let the sharing be a conscious choice rather than a habitual reaction.

Furthermore, work on honing your listening skills. Mysterious individuals are often excellent listeners, which helps them engage in meaningful conversations without revealing much about themselves. Active listening allows you to contribute to discussions and build connections, all while maintaining your mysterious allure.

Another strategy is to pursue unique interests or unconventional hobbies. Sigma males often have eclectic tastes that deviate from the mainstream. Having such interests not only makes you more intriguing but also enriches your personality and makes you more self-contented.

Finally, strive for independence in all aspects of your life. The self-reliance of sigma males significantly contributes to their mysterious aura. When you're not constantly seeking others' help or approval, you naturally project an aura of self-sufficiency that others find intriguing.

In essence, cultivating a mysterious aura involves balancing solitude and social engagements, being thoughtful in personal disclosures, listening actively, nurturing unique interests, and fostering independence. As we emphasize these traits, remember that the goal is not to become elusive or aloof but to cultivate an authentic and captivating persona that reflects your true self.

In the next chapter, titled 'The Silent Influencer,' we will explore how sigma males, despite their quiet demeanour, often become powerful influencers. They influence not through loud proclamations or charisma, but through their actions, integrity, and unique perspectives. How can one wield influence silently, and why is it a strength of the sigma male? We'll discuss these questions and more as we delve deeper into the sigma male archetype.

Chapter 49: The Silent Influencer

Sigma males are known as silent influencers due to their quiet yet powerful impact on others. They don't rely on loud proclamations, authoritative leadership, or the charisma typically associated with leadership. Instead, their influence lies in their actions, integrity, unique perspectives, and the subtlety of their interactions. Let's understand this trait more deeply and explore how one can adopt this form of influence.

Sigma males influence silently through the example they set for others. Their self-reliance, resilience, and independence make them role models in their personal and professional circles. They don't need to voice their ideals or principles loudly; instead, they live them. It's this authenticity and consistency that make them influential.

For instance, consider the example of a team leader who works diligently, adheres strictly to ethics, and respects everyone's opinions. He doesn't make grand speeches or boast about his accomplishments. Instead, he leads by example, inspiring his team to emulate his work ethic and values. His quiet demeanour does not diminish his impact; it enhances it, setting him apart from more vocal leaders and making his influence more significant.

On the other hand, think of a friend who, instead of offering unsolicited advice, supports you by being a reliable presence and demonstrating through their actions how they handle adversity. Their silent support and example could inspire you to handle your challenges more effectively.

So how can one adopt the sigma trait of being a silent influencer?

Firstly, focus on actions over words. Sigma males understand that actions speak louder than words. Ensure that your actions align with your values and principles. Be consistent in your behaviour and allow your actions to communicate your values.

Next, be authentic. Sigma males are influential because they are true to themselves. Authenticity breeds trust, and people are more likely to be influenced by someone they trust. Don't try to be someone you're not; embrace your uniqueness and allow your genuine self to shine through.

Practice active listening. Being a silent influencer does not mean being completely silent. It means talking less and listening more. Active listening helps you understand others better, enabling you to provide the right support or guidance when needed.

Embrace humility. Sigma males do not seek constant recognition or applause. They are content knowing they've acted according to their values. This humble attitude makes their influence more potent, as it's clear they're guided by principles rather than a desire for personal gain.

Lastly, work on building resilience and self-reliance. These are core traits of sigma males and major contributors to their silent influence. Resilience helps you navigate life's ups and downs effectively, and self-reliance ensures you are not overly dependent on others. Both these qualities, when observed, can greatly influence and inspire those around you.

In adopting these practices, remember that being a silent influencer isn't about suppressing your voice. It's about understanding the power of subtlety and action. It's about leading by example and knowing when to speak and when to let your actions do the talking.

In the upcoming chapter, we will discuss another key sigma trait: adaptability. This trait makes sigma males versatile and resilient in the face of change and adversity. We will understand what adaptability truly means and how sigma males embody this trait. We'll also provide practical advice on how you can cultivate adaptability in your own life. Stay tuned to delve deeper into the unique world of sigma males.

Chapter 50: Adapting to Change - The Sigma Male Way

The ability to adapt to change is a key trait of a sigma male, making them resilient, flexible, and uniquely equipped to navigate through life's ever-changing circumstances. In this chapter, we'll explore this trait in depth, share some relatable examples, and offer practical advice on how to cultivate it in your own life.

Sigma males are often seen as solitary figures who prefer to navigate life independently. However, their solitary nature does not make them rigid. On the contrary, their independence cultivates a remarkable ability to adapt to new situations. They can navigate various social contexts, environments, and challenges with an almost chameleon-like ability, adjusting their approach as needed while staying true to their core principles and goals.

Take the example of a sigma male who works as a freelancer. In the world of freelancing, the ability to adapt is vital. Our sigma freelancer might work with different clients, each with different expectations and styles of communication. One week, he could be designing a website for a local restaurant. The next, he might be writing code for an ambitious tech startup. Despite these constant shifts, he thrives, adjusting his working style, interaction, and even his learning, to deliver the best results for his clients.

On a personal front, consider a sigma male who moves to a new city or even a new country. The new environment could be vastly different, and integrating into a new culture can be challenging. But the sigma male takes these changes in stride, learning the local language, understanding the cultural nuances, and making new connections, all while maintaining his own identity and principles.

So how does one develop this sigma trait of adaptability?

Firstly, cultivate an open mind. Sigma males do not resist change; they embrace it. They understand that change is a part of life and often brings opportunities for growth. By keeping an open mind, you allow yourself to see the potential that change can bring.

Secondly, be proactive in learning. Sigma males are often autodidacts, learning independently out of curiosity or necessity. In a world that's constantly changing, being a proactive learner can help you keep up and adapt.

Next, focus on problem-solving. Sigma males are often adept at finding solutions to the challenges they face. Developing good problem-solving skills can help you adapt to new situations, as you'll be able to identify potential issues and navigate around them effectively.

Also, remember to be patient with yourself. Adapting to change can take time, and that's okay. Sigma males understand this, which is why they do not rush the process. They give themselves time to adjust, learn, and grow.

Finally, maintain a strong sense of self. While sigma males can adapt to different situations, they never lose sight of who they are. They adapt their approach, not their principles. Keeping your core values intact while adapting to change can help you navigate life's twists and turns while staying true to yourself.

Developing adaptability doesn't mean you have to lose your identity or become a different person. Rather, it's about learning how to adjust your approach to meet different circumstances while remaining authentic to your values and goals.

As we bring this chapter to a close, it is time to reflect on the journey we've taken through the fascinating world of sigma males. We've delved into various sigma traits - their independence, introspection, self-reliance, silent influence, and adaptability, among others. We've explored what each trait means, how sigma males embody them, and how you can incorporate these traits into your own life.

In the next and final chapter, we will summarize our exploration into the world of the sigma male. We will reflect on the unique traits that define them and the invaluable lessons we can learn from this distinctive personality archetype. We'll also revisit how you can adopt these traits to enhance your own personal growth journey. So, stay tuned as we tie together the threads of our exploration and conclude this comprehensive guide to understanding and adopting the traits of a sigma male.

Conclusion: Sigma Male Traits - A Journey Towards Personal Mastery

Over the course of this comprehensive guide, we've explored in depth the world of the sigma male, a personality archetype that defies convention and offers valuable insights into personal growth and self-improvement. This concluding chapter serves as a summary and a reflection on our journey, pulling together the key insights and takeaways from each chapter, and how you can incorporate these into your own life to become the best version of yourself.

In the early chapters, we introduced the sigma male archetype, a person who is independent, introverted, and self-reliant. We discovered that sigma males aren't defined by societal norms or expectations, but rather by their personal values and goals. They prefer solitude over unnecessary social interactions, finding peace and fulfilment in their own company. They're often introspective, using solitude to reflect on their lives, make meaningful decisions, and chart their own course.

We also explored their unique approach to personal success. Unlike alpha males, who tend to be dominant and seek to lead, sigma males are not driven by a need for external validation or status. Instead, they focus on achieving their personal goals and ideals. We looked at the example of a sigma male artist, who creates art not for fame or recognition, but because it fulfils him and aligns with his values.

As we delved deeper, we uncovered the ways sigma males influence their environment. Even though they often choose to remain in the background, they can have a profound impact on those around them through their actions and by leading by example. We considered the case of the sigma male environmentalist who, through his actions, inspires others to live more sustainably.

We then turned our attention to sigma males' resilience and adaptability, qualities that equip them to deal effectively with life's challenges and changes. Whether it's a freelancer juggling various projects or someone integrating into a new culture, the sigma male thrives on flexibility and adaptation.

In each chapter, we didn't just describe these traits but also explored ways to incorporate them into our own lives. We encouraged cultivating solitude, introspection, self-reliance, personal success, silent influence, resilience, and adaptability. By adopting these traits, we can become more attuned to our own needs, values, and goals, and lead a life that's more authentic and fulfilling.

As we conclude this guide, the main takeaway is this: being a sigma male is about embracing your uniqueness, following your own path, and staying true to your values. It's about not conforming for the sake of fitting in, but having the courage to stand apart. It's about finding strength in solitude, peace in introspection, and satisfaction in self-reliance.

However, it's important to remember that the aim is not to fit into a specific mold or archetype, but to glean insights that resonate with us and enrich our personal growth journey. Whether you identify with every trait of a sigma male, or just a few, the goal is personal mastery, self-understanding, and authentic living.

In a world that often praises extraversion, dominance, and social hierarchy, the sigma male stands as a testament to the power of introspection, quiet strength, and personal fulfilment. It reminds us that success and happiness are highly personal and subjective, and that the quiet, introspective, and non-conformist path is just as valid and rewarding.

In conclusion, the traits of the sigma male offer valuable lessons for anyone seeking to navigate life on their own terms. As we wrap up this guide, I hope you carry these insights with you, apply them in your life, and embark on a journey towards personal mastery that is as unique and authentic as you are.

Printed in Great Britain
by Amazon